DORLING KINDERSLEY [DK] EYEWITNESS BOOKS

FLAG

Japanese naval ensign from World War II, with Rising Sun design

Bunting

Chinese flag, 19th century, with figure of winged tiger

British heraldic crest with flag

DK EYEWITNESS BOOKS

FLAG

Written by
WILLIAM CRAMPTON

Dice from early
20th-century flag game

...es from
...d War I, showing flags
...ance, Great Britain, and Belgium

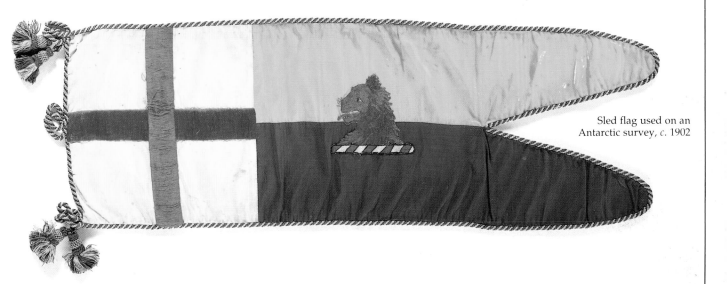

Sled flag used on an
Antarctic survey, c. 1902

Dorling Kindersley

Plastic marker flags
used in sports events

Olive branches,
common symbol of peace

Chinese nationalist
flag of the 1920s

British heraldic shield

DK

Dorling Kindersley
LONDON, NEW YORK, DELHI, JOHANNESBURG,
MUNICH, PARIS and SYDNEY

For a full catalog, visit

DK www.dk.com

Project editor Phil Wilkinson
Art editor Peter Bailey
Senior editor Sophie Mitchell
Senior art editor Julia Harris
Managing art editor Roger Priddy
Managing editor Sue Unstead
Consultant Jos Poels

This Eyewitness ® Book has been conceived by
Dorling Kindersley Limited and Editions Gallimard

© 1989 Dorling Kindersley Limited
This edition © 2000 Dorling Kindersley Limited
First American edition, 1989

Published in the United States by
Dorling Kindersley Publishing, Inc.
95 Madison Avenue
New York, NY 10016
2 4 6 8 10 9 7 5 3 1

Dorling Kindersley books are available at special discounts for bulk
purchases for sales promotions or premiums. Special editions,
including personalized covers, excerpts of existing guides, and
corporate imprints can be created in large quantities for specific
needs. For more information, contact Special Markets Dept., Dorling
Kindersley Publishing, Inc., 95 Madison Ave., New York, NY 10016;
Fax: (800) 600-9098

Badge showing of Spain

Stamp with flag of
Chinese Liberation A

Library of Congress Cataloging-in-Publication Data
Crampton, W. G. (William G.)
Flag / written by William Crampton;
photography by Karl Shone and Martin Plomer.
p. cm. — (Eyewitness Books)
Includes index.
Summary: A photographic essay about flags from countries all over the
world and such special flags as signal flags for ships and boats, flags for
special festivals and sports, political flags, and coats of arms. Also
includes information about the meaning of shapes and colors on flags.
1. Flags — Juvenile literature. [Flags.]
I. Shone, Karl, ill. II. Plomer, Martin, ill. III. Title.
CR109.C72 2000 929.9'2 — dc19 88-27174
ISBN 0-7894-5825-X (pb)
ISBN 0-7894-5824-1 (hc)

Color reproduction by Colourscan, Singapore
Printed in China by Toppan Printing Co. (Shenzhen) Ltd.

Army car penn

Seal of King Edward VII

Flag flown over headquarters
of a commando unit during
World War II

Flag of Gazelle Force,
a British unit in the Sudan, 1940

Contents

Selection of flag badges

France, Britain, and Belgium

Canada, Britain, Australia, USA, New Zealand

Soviet flags

Palestine

Salvation Army

The anatomy of a flag

F<small>LAGS COME IN ALL SHAPES AND SIZES</small>. Usually they consist of a piece of free-flying fabric attached to a rigid vertical staff, but they may also be hung from horizontal bars. Flags may be flown from flagpoles or the halyards of sailing ships, carried on staves or spears, fixed on pins for table stands, or hung from spars at 45 degrees to the vertical (known as gaffs). Most modern flags are made from polyester. Many different fabrics have been used in the past, including silk, taffeta, cotton, linen, and wool. The designs may be built up by sewing together material of different colors, or they may be printed. In the past, elaborate designs were often painted or embroidered onto the surface of the flag, and these methods are sometimes still used today. Since the 17th century most of the flags used at sea have been rectangular, and this is now the standard form for use on land. Military flags are traditionally square. Some flags flown by yachts are swallow-tailed or triangular, and heraldic banners (pp.10-11) are squarish.

British flag makers producing flags in the early 1950s.

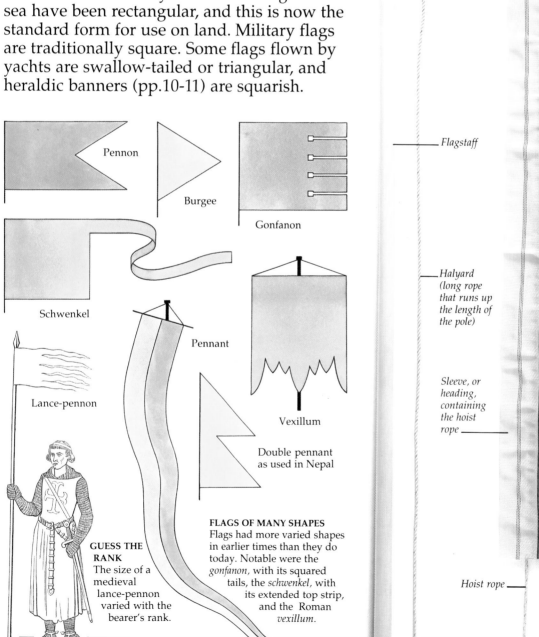

Pennon

Burgee

Gonfanon

Schwenkel

Pennant

Vexillum

Lance-pennon

Double pennant as used in Nepal

GUESS THE RANK
The size of a medieval lance-pennon varied with the bearer's rank.

FLAGS OF MANY SHAPES
Flags had more varied shapes in earlier times than they do today. Notable were the *gonfanon*, with its squared tails, the *schwenkel*, with its extended top strip, and the Roman *vexillum*.

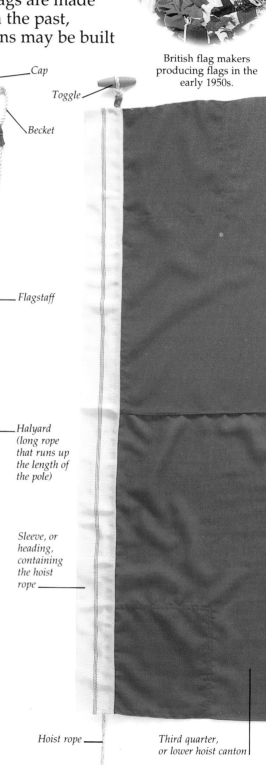

Cap

Toggle

Becket

Flagstaff

Halyard (long rope that runs up the length of the pole)

Sleeve, or heading, containing the hoist rope

Hoist rope

Third quarter, or lower hoist canton

THE MONGOL CONQUEROR
This is a traditional view of the banner of the Mongol leader Ghengis Khan, with a flag of nine "feet" beneath four horse tails. Chinese flags also had elaborately decorated ragged edges and colored borders, but rarely contained emblems such as the hawk of the Mongols.

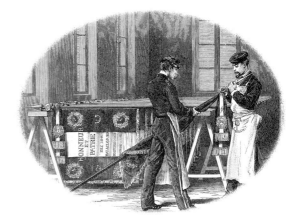

MILITARY DECORATIONS
French military flags follow set patterns and are decorated with gold fringes and cravats (decorative streamers) attached just beneath the finial of the flagstaff. These carry the unit's number, as well as any honors that it has been awarded.

Second quarter, or upper fly canton

THE PARTS OF A FLAG
Flags are divided into four quarters, or *cantons*. The two nearest the pole form the *hoist* and the other two the *fly*. The upper canton of the hoist, which often contains a badge or emblem, is also often known simply as the *canton*. Flags to be flown from a pole have a hollow tube of cloth called a *sleeve*, or *heading*, on the hoist side. Those made in Europe usually have a *hoist rope* sewn into this; American flags have an eyelet at either end. For indoor or parade use the flagstaff is passed through the heading, and ropes and tassels are often attached to the decorative *finial* at the end of the pole. The horizontal dimension (size) of a flag is the *length* and the vertical dimension is the *width*. The proportions of a flag are shown by two numbers, the first refering to the height of the flag and the second to the width. So a flag 1 ft high and 2 ft wide is in proportions of 1:2.

FOLDING THE FLAG
Military flags are hoisted (raised), lowered, folded, and stored according to set rules and rituals.

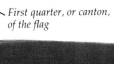
First quarter, or canton, of the flag

Becket

Pulley

Finial

Toggle

Looped clips

Inglefield clips

Fourth quarter, or lower fly canton

FLYING FLAGS
There are various ways of fastening flags to the staff. American flags have eyelets to which clips are attached. In England the hoist rope is usually attached to the halyard with a becket and toggle. Inglefield clips (with their quick-release mechanism) are often used at sea. Indoor and parade flagstaffs have elaborate finials.

First signs

WE USUALLY THINK OF A FLAG as a piece of fabric attached to a pole. But before flags as we know them were invented, people carried poles topped with carved symbols. They used these objects in the same way that we use flags today - to send signals or to show loyalty to a leader or country. The first evidence of these solid flaglike objects comes from ancient Egypt, where they were used to identify various parts of the kingdom. The ancient civilizations of Greece, Rome, and the Middle East used them in similar ways. It was the ancient Romans who made most use of the symbols. Each unit of their army had its own "standard", including the famous eagles of the legions. They also introduced the first true flag in the Western world - the *vexillum*. Unlike modern flags it was attached to a horizontal pole. Flags attached along one side to an upright pole first appeared in China, and were introduced to the west by the Arabs. But even then, flags were usually made only of plain fabric. Flags with actual designs on them became widespread during the Crusades (11th-13th centuries). The Christians used the symbol of the cross; the Moslems carried flags bearing inscriptions. In America, the Aztecs had developed flags made of feathers and also had flags that could be carried on a warrior's back.

EVIDENCE FROM EGYPT
This ancient Egyptian pot comes from the predynastic period (before 3000 B.C.). The object at the end of the pole on the right-hand side of the pot is a very early image of a flaglike object called a vexilloid.

HOMEMADE FLAG
The first flag was probably no more than a piece of cloth tied to a stick, but it could still be used to attract attention or to send a message. Natural dyes could produce very bright colors, like on this red flag. A plain flag still means danger today, just as it did in prehistoric times.

FLAG OR FAN?
The ancient Egyptians had vexilloids that could be carried or fixed on chariots. Some looked like fans; others consisted of carvings attached to poles.

BULL OF THE ASSYRIANS
The ancient Assyrians were a people who had a large empire in the Middle East. They were involved in many military campaigns and had standards bearing figures of an archer on a bull's back and of two bulls. The standards were usually carried by charioteers.

ROMAN STANDARDS
The standards carried by Roman military units varied in design but all bore medals and badges. These two examples incorporate a vexillum (see below), which would have been a special award, and a hand to ward off the evil eye. Other badges used by the Romans included portraits of the emperor, laurel wreaths, and crowns.

Finial on top of pole could contain legion badge

STREET IN CHINA
Chinese flags took a variety of forms, including ones like fans and streamers. Most relied on color for their effect, rather than detailed designs.

Painted figure

Silver ornaments

PRIDE OF A LEGION
This is a modern reconstruction of the Roman vexillum, the first true flag. It was the flag of a particular part of a legion, and was designed to be carried on horseback. The flag was a square of dark red cloth, and the original could have had a picture or an inscription on it.

Name of legion

LEG II AVG

Coats of arms

The basis of a coat of arms is the shield. This one is from a ceiling in a 15th-century building.

Heraldry is the art of producing and recording coats of arms. It has had a great influence on flags, creating new kinds of flags and laying down ground rules for their design and use. Anyone who has a coat of arms can also use heraldic flags. Traditionally these are the long *standard*, the rectangular *banner*, the *badge-flag*, and the *pennon*. A coat of arms consists of the following items: a shield, which can contain symbols connected to the history of the bearer's family; *supporters* on either side of the shield; and a helmet with a wreath, mantling (cloth hanging from the helmet), and a *crest* on top of the shield. There may be a scroll and a motto. Arms and heraldic flags are granted to one person only, and may not be used by anyone else.

STAMP OF APPROVAL
Personal heraldry - and heraldry of towns and cities - can be displayed on seals. Sometimes the whole coat of arms is shown; sometimes there is an image of the bearer of the arms in full heraldic armor.

Wreath, or "torse," in the "livery colors" of the arms

Crest always stands on top of wreath, or "torse"

Helmet of the kind used in medieval tournaments

STANDARDS
Heraldic standards show the colors, arms badges, and mottoes of the bearer. The bearers' shields are shown alongside.

FOR DISPLAY
This helmet is not designed to be worn - it comes from a coat of arms and bears a wreath and crest. The double-headed eagle of the crest also bears a cross, as does the highly decorated helmet.

KNIGHTS OF OLD
Tournaments were great occasions for displays of heraldry and usually included an exhibition of the armor, coats of arms, and banners of those taking part.

YAL ARMS

the time of Henry VIII the British royal coat rms had the lion of England and the Red gon of Wales (one of the badges of the Tudor asty) as "supporters."

Churchill arms

"Cadency mark" to indicate a second son

Spencer arms

FOR A NATIONAL HERO

In Sir Winston Churchill's heraldic banner the background is the same as the shield of the coat of arms, and the border of black and white is in the main colors of the arms. The arms incorporate those of Churchill's two lines of descent, the families of Churchill and Spencer.

Cloves

Tree peony

EASTERN SYMBOLS

Japanese heraldry uses highly stylized family badges known as *mon*. These can be borne on flags, used for decoration, or included on fans and clothing. Unlike European heraldic devices they do not have specific colors.

KNIGHT IN ARMOR

Sir John Cornwall was an English knight of the 15th century. He is depicted with his coat of arms, heraldic standard, and a surcoat bearing his crest. The soldier behind him is carrying a standard bearing the arms of a member of the royal family of the period.

Royal standard

Surcoat

Standard of Sir John Cornwall

Shield

Wreath

Churchill's crest is a lion bearing a flag. It is very unusual for heraldic crests to incorporate flags in this way. The heraldic term for the pose in which the lion is shown is *sejant* (seated) with one paw raised.

Friend or foe?

IN THE CONFUSION OF THE BATTLEFIELD, flags provide an easy method of telling friends from enemies. Flags were once a common sight wherever battles raged, and even today they are used by the military, both on land and at sea. In medieval times (the 15th century) they identified individuals as well groups, in the way that flags on vehicles and flags that fly over battle headquarters still do today. When armies became more organized (from the 16th century on), each individual regiment and company developed its own flag. These were known as colors, and they were often elaborately decorated with embroidered coats of arms. Eventually colors were used only in ceremonies - sturdier flags were needed for battle.

COMING OF THE CONQUEROR
The Norman knights at the Battle of Hastings in 1066 carried small flags called *pennons* on their lances. Duke William had an elaborate one sent to him by the Pope.

WHO WAS WHO?
Medieval knights were easily identified because they carried their personal emblems on their shields and banners.

Initials of the Ringwood Light Dragoons

Royal monogram of King George III

THE CAVALRY ARE COMING
A descendant of the medieval lance-pennon is the cavalry guidon. This one dates from the Napoleonic Wars (1796-1815) and was meant to be carried on horseback.

Royal badge of the White Horse of Hanover

Lancer with pennon attached to his lance

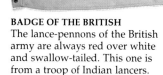

Sleeve could be nailed to the lance

Very deep swallowtail

BADGE OF THE BRITISH
The lance-pennons of the British army are always red over white and swallow-tailed. This one is from a troop of Indian lancers.

LANCERS
Lances were still used after firearms were invented. A famous example was the ill-fated Charge of the Light Brigade in the Crimean War (1853-56), in which many British lancers died.

...FIC OVERTURES
...World War II poster represents
...rican victories over the Japanese.

THE SWASTIKA
The Nazi swastika is one of
the best-known political symbols
of modern times. Originally a
sun symbol, it was used in many
different ways before it became
the national flag of Germany in
1935. This version was used as a
wall hanging. The swastika
flag was replaced in 1945
(pp. 28-29).

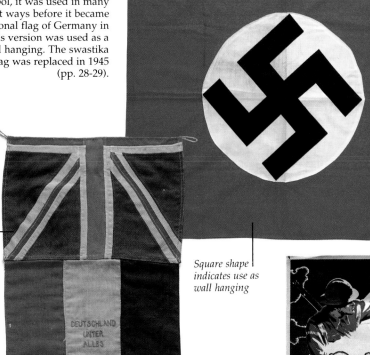

*Square shape
indicates use as
wall hanging*

Union Jack

PROPAGANDA FLAG
This flag, made during
World War I, shows the
German national flag of
the period beneath the
Union Jack (p. 47). The
motto *Deutschland unter
Alles* ("Germany under
all") pokes fun at a
phrase from the German
national anthem.

DEUTSCHLAND
UNTER
ALLES

German flag

ONE WAR
The slogan on this poster from
World War II means "One
struggle for one country."

UN SEUL COMBAT
POUR UNE SEULE PATRIE

LIBERTÉ
ÉGALITÉ
FRATERNITÉ

SIDE BY SIDE
The United States, France,
England, and Italy are among the
World War I Allies shown here.
The flagstaffs are topped by
decorative finials, a common
feature of military flags.

*The flags of
Britain, France,
and Belgium*

Japan
(the Rising Sun)

*The arms
and flag
of Belgium*

Russia (the
Naval Ensign)

France

Britain

Belgium

...GS FOR ALL
...ces showing the
...d flags of the Allies
... very common during
...d War II. They took
...riety of forms,
...ding badges,
...kerchiefs, scarves,
...s, and games.

FLAG GAME
This game consists of
dice with a different
flag on each face.

FRIEND IN NEED
Flags can still be used for
identification in modern
warfare. They are especially
useful because they are
international symbols that
anyone can understand. This piece of cloth was designed to be
carried by British pilots serving in Eastern Europe during World
War II. It bears the message "I am British" and an instruction to
contact the local British Military Mission.

Я англичанин

"Ya Anglicháhnin" *(Pronounced as spelt)*

Пожалуйста сообщите
сведения обо мне в
Британскую Военную
Миссию в Москве

Please
communicate
my particulars
to British
Military Mission
Moscow

Showing your colors

Mᴀɴʏ ꜰʟᴀɢꜱ ɪɴᴄʟᴜᴅᴇ ꜱʏᴍʙᴏʟꜱ that are used to express ideas which would otherwise take many words. These symbols come from many different sources – from animals, plants, weapons, and everyday objects. One of the best-known examples is the lion in medieval heraldry, which represented both kingship and bravery. Colors are also given symbolic meanings. We use white and blue to represent peace in flags like that of the United Nations. And green is the color of vegetation but has also been used to represent youth and hope. Religious ideas are among the oldest to be expressed in flag form, and the cross is the oldest device in heraldry. In Moslem countries (where Islam is practiced) the crescent moon has been a symbol of religion since at least the 14th century; the crescent combined with a star is not as old. Another Islamic symbol is the double-bladed sword, which represents the Prophet's son-in-law, Ali. Islamic law does not allow pictures of God or people, but other religions have no such restrictions and there are many Chinese flags that show gods and Christian flags that show images of saints. Modern symbols include the Canadian maple leaf and the hammer and sickle of the former Soviet Union.

Hammer and sickle

Flag of former USSR

WORKERS UNITE!
The tools of the industrial and the agricultural labourer (the "workers" and "peasants" of the Russian Revolution) appeared in styl form on the flag of the former Soviet

WELLINGTON'S CREST
The combination of the king of beasts with the flag of victory rising from a duke's crown forms a fitting crest for the Duke of Wellington.

HOLY WAR?
In this illustration of tribal warfare in 19th-century Morocco, the green Islamic flag stands out.

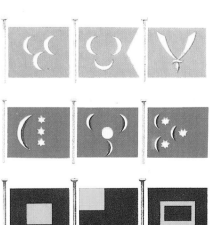

WHICH COLOR?
These flags show how colors can have special meanings. Red and green were often used by Islamic countries in the 19th century. The green flags show forms of the crescent used in the Ottoman Empire, and the sword of Ali on the flag of a North African port. The red flags come from Turkey, India, and Egypt. The blue and yellow flags are "matricu-lation" flags, used in the 19th century to show a ship's port of registration.

Flag of Canada

Red maple leaf

CANADIAN MAPLE
For ease of manufacture and reproduction the red maple leaf on the flag of Canada has been reduced to a highly stylized form, making a new heraldic emblem. This has happened to all the devices used in flags and coats of arms.

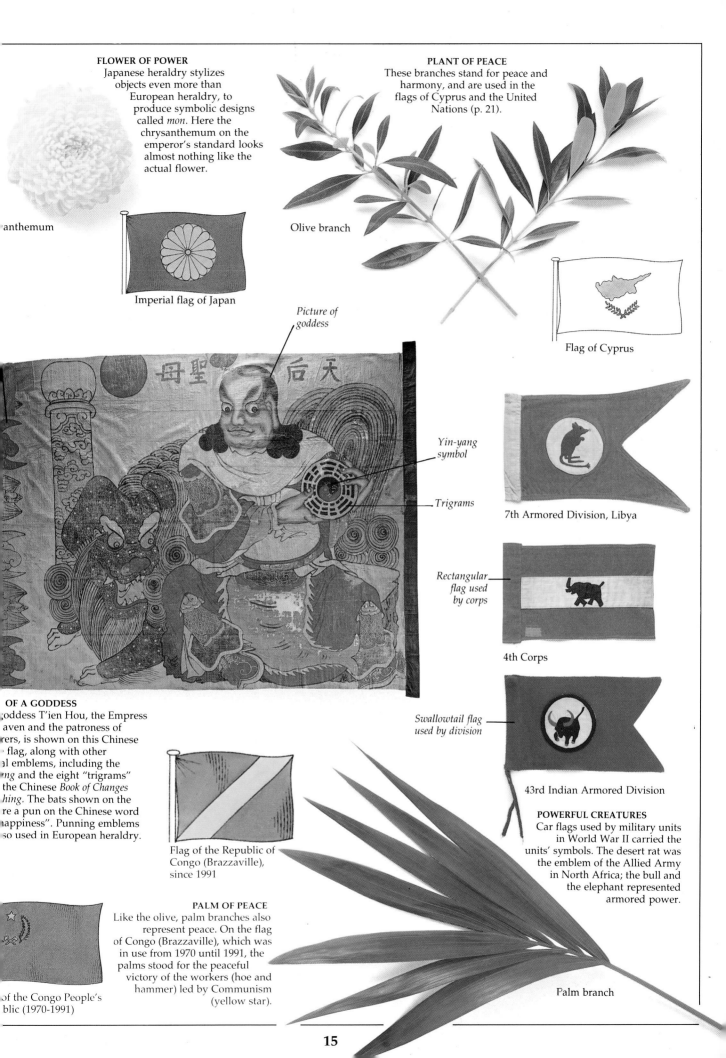

FLOWER OF POWER
Japanese heraldry stylizes objects even more than European heraldry, to produce symbolic designs called *mon*. Here the chrysanthemum on the emperor's standard looks almost nothing like the actual flower.

...anthemum

Imperial flag of Japan

PLANT OF PEACE
These branches stand for peace and harmony, and are used in the flags of Cyprus and the United Nations (p. 21).

Olive branch

Flag of Cyprus

Picture of goddess

Yin-yang symbol

Trigrams

7th Armored Division, Libya

Rectangular flag used by corps

4th Corps

Swallowtail flag used by division

43rd Indian Armored Division

...OF A GODDESS
...oddess T'ien Hou, the Empress ...aven and the patroness of ...rers, is shown on this Chinese ... flag, along with other ...al emblems, including the ...*ng* and the eight "trigrams" ... the Chinese *Book of Changes* ...*hing*. The bats shown on the ...re a pun on the Chinese word ...appiness". Punning emblems ...so used in European heraldry.

Flag of the Republic of Congo (Brazzaville), since 1991

PALM OF PEACE
Like the olive, palm branches also represent peace. On the flag of Congo (Brazzaville), which was in use from 1970 until 1991, the palms stood for the peaceful victory of the workers (hoe and hammer) led by Communism (yellow star).

...of the Congo People's ...blic (1970-1991)

POWERFUL CREATURES
Car flags used by military units in World War II carried the units' symbols. The desert rat was the emblem of the Allied Army in North Africa; the bull and the elephant represented armored power.

Palm branch

Setting sail

Sᴉɴᴄᴇ ᴛʜᴇ ᴅᴀʏs ᴏꜰ ᴛʜᴇ ꜰɪʀsᴛ ᴡᴀʀsʜɪᴘs and the earliest trading vessels, flags have always been used at sea. Today such ships - as well as the thousands of passenger ships and the boats of all shapes and sizes that are used for recreation - still use flags. All ships over a certain size are supposed to display their natio colors, although many do not do so. In practice this means that they should fly their national or mercantil (commercial) flag or naval ensign. The Stars and Stripes plays all these roles for American ships; Britisl ships fly one of the three British Ensigns. About twent other nations are like England in having separate national and mercantile flags, and one or two have separate national flags for yachts. In addition, commercial shipping lines display their individual company flags. Other flag traditions include flying the proper national flag whe entering a foreign port - this is known as flying a "courtesy flag." On leaving port, many sh fly the blue flag with a white square in the cen called the Blue Peter.

DRESSED OVERALL
On holidays and when celebrating important victories, ships used to fly all their available flags, producing an effect like this. Today only signal flags are used to "dress ship."

Material is orange damask silk

Yin-yang symbol representing the coming together of opposites

Trigrams from the I Ching

PHILOSOPHICAL FLAG
This pennant comes from a Chinese junk (sailboat). It illustrates some of the key ideas in traditional Chinese thought, with the yin-yang symbol at the hoist and the trigrams from the *Book of Changes* or *I Ching* prominently displayed along the length of the flag. The pennant also has a ragged edge, typical of Chinese flags.

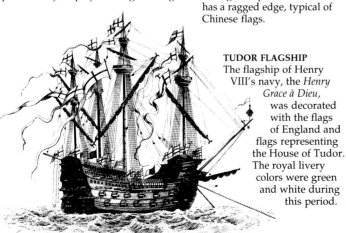

TUDOR FLAGSHIP
The flagship of Henry VIII's navy, the *Henry Grace à Dieu*, was decorated with the flags of England and flags representing the House of Tudor. The royal livery colors were green and white during this period.

BRITISH ENSIG
The White Ensi
the form of the
British nationa
flag used exclu
ly on ships of t
Royal Navy. Th
Red and Blue
Ensigns are als
British national
flags for use at
the first for civi
vessels and the
second for ship
government se

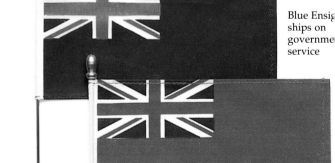

Blue Ensig
ships on
governme
service

Red Ensign for
civilian vessels

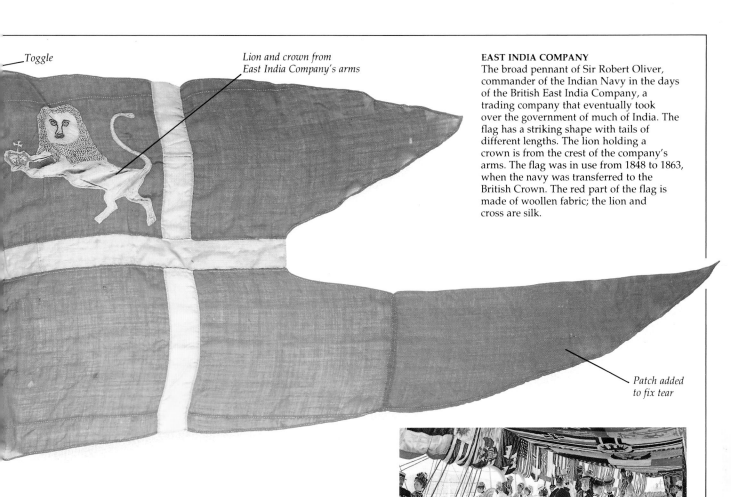

Toggle

Lion and crown from East India Company's arms

EAST INDIA COMPANY
The broad pennant of Sir Robert Oliver, commander of the Indian Navy in the days of the British East India Company, a trading company that eventually took over the government of much of India. The flag has a striking shape with tails of different lengths. The lion holding a crown is from the crest of the company's arms. The flag was in use from 1848 to 1863, when the navy was transferred to the British Crown. The red part of the flag is made of woollen fabric; the lion and cross are silk.

Patch added to fix tear

Hoist rope

FROM THE CHINA SEAS
The shape and design of this flag from a Chinese junk are typical of the flags of the China Sea in the last century. The main motif is a dragon, and the inscriptions can be translated as "Lord of Suiyan" and "Spirit Banner."

BALL ON SHIPBOARD
In this oil painting of a ball on board ship (_c._ 1874) the deck is canopied with the contents of the ship's flag locker, including several royal standards and national flags. Using flags in this way today would be considered disrespectful.

Typical ragged (or "invected") border, with lightning flashes

侯 遠 駿
神
生
顯

Material is silk damask with gold appliqué

LE COLORS
66 the Italians and Prussians fought Austria. In this
re of one of the battles, long pennants and national
ignaling flags can be seen.

Hollow linen sleeve for mounting on bamboo pole

Signaling with flags

SIGNALING AT SEA is one of the oldest uses of flags. Signals were sent with flaglike objects called vexilloids (pp. 8-9) by both sides in the wars between the Greeks and Persians (547-478 BC). By the Middle Ages the Genoese and Venetian fleets of Italy had more elaborate signals. The first specially made signal flag was the "Banner of the Council" introduced for the English fleet in 13 (used to summon captains to the admiral's ship). Signals were als sent by hoisting ordinary flags in special positions. The first regular code of flag signals dates from the seventeenth century in England. In the following century numeral flags were invented; they could be combined to make up messages. Each ship also had pennants to represent its name, and the numbers could also represent letters of the alphabet. In 1812 Sir Home Popham introduced special flags for letters of the alphabet and by 1889 there was a flag for each letter and numeral. The first International Code of Signals was introduced on January 1, 1901. Flag signaling, with semaphore and other flags, is also used on land.

COURTESY FLAG
A ship about to enter a foreign port hoists the flag of that country as a courtesy (p. 16).

619

CODE OF SIGNALS
This is flag 19, the letter O (Oscar), from the International Code of Signals. As well as representing the letters of the alphabet, the flags also indicate a particular message. This one represents the signal "Man overboard." Signal flags are usually made in proportions of 5:6.

Pair of semaphore flags

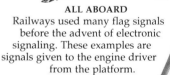

ALL ABOARD
Railways used many flag signals before the advent of electronic signaling. These examples are signals given to the engine driver from the platform.

SEMAPHORE
The semaphore system of signaling involves changing the positions of both arms to represent different letters and numbers. This is the semaphore signal for the letter C.

MORSE CODE
During the American Civil War, a signaling method was developed that used a single flag to represent the dots and dashes of the Morse code.

The letter E in the flag semaphore code.

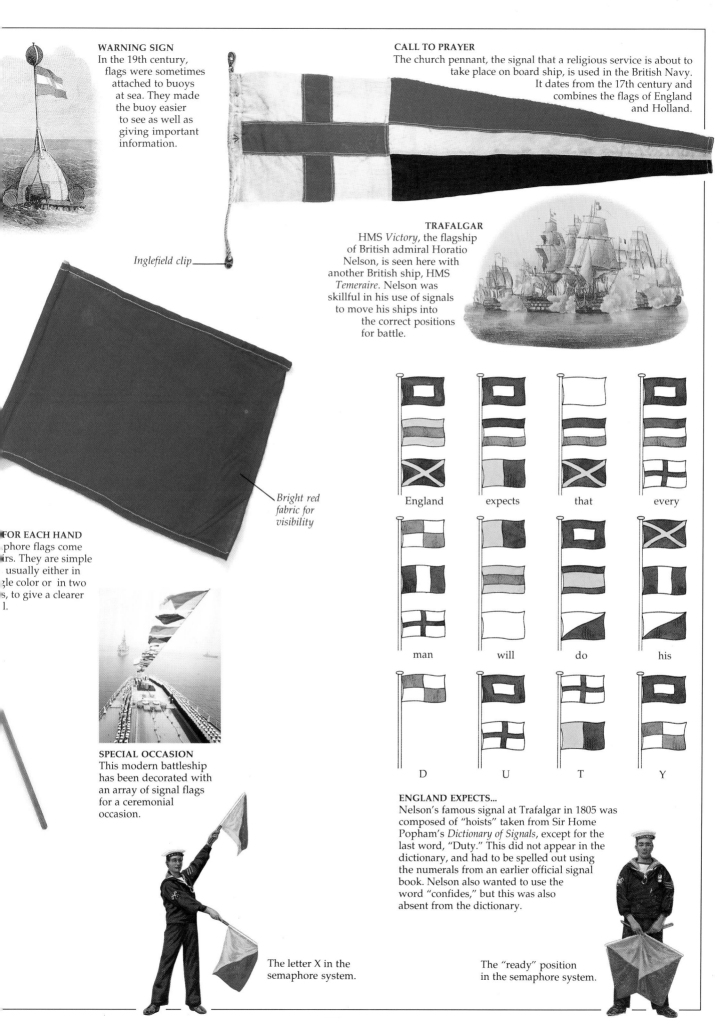

WARNING SIGN
In the 19th century, flags were sometimes attached to buoys at sea. They made the buoy easier to see as well as giving important information.

CALL TO PRAYER
The church pennant, the signal that a religious service is about to take place on board ship, is used in the British Navy. It dates from the 17th century and combines the flags of England and Holland.

Inglefield clip

TRAFALGAR
HMS *Victory*, the flagship of British admiral Horatio Nelson, is seen here with another British ship, HMS *Temeraire*. Nelson was skillful in his use of signals to move his ships into the correct positions for battle.

Bright red fabric for visibility

FOR EACH HAND
phore flags come
irs. They are simple
usually either in
zle color or in two
s, to give a clearer
l.

SPECIAL OCCASION
This modern battleship has been decorated with an array of signal flags for a ceremonial occasion.

England expects that every

man will do his

D U T Y

ENGLAND EXPECTS...
Nelson's famous signal at Trafalgar in 1805 was composed of "hoists" taken from Sir Home Popham's *Dictionary of Signals*, except for the last word, "Duty." This did not appear in the dictionary, and had to be spelled out using the numerals from an earlier official signal book. Nelson also wanted to use the word "confides," but this was also absent from the dictionary.

The letter X in the semaphore system.

The "ready" position in the semaphore system.

Flags of the people

LAMB AND FLAG
This was an enduring religious symbol in the Middle Ages.

MANY FLAGS START LIFE being locally designed and made by individua in response to the need for symbols of religious, political, or social action. Such flag designers do not always pay attention to the strict rules of heraldry or of flag design, and so the flags they produce are usually quickly and simply made. They often include very simple symbols (like the crab from the Southern Cameroons, a region in Africa, shown opposite) and many also have some sort of inscription (whether a religious text or a political slogan). Some go on to become well-established political or national flags; others exist only for the moment. They are often subject to local changes and variations and are rarely made in a standard form. But this seldom matters to their users because, unlike national flags, they are more often used to rally the faithful than for identification.

SWAPO f

ANC flag

Early 20 century Armeni flag

FOR LIBERTY
The tricolor ornament is visible in this scene from the time of the French Revolution (pp. 26-27).

FLAGS OF STRUGGLE
Groups fighting to free their country from foreign rule ofter their emblems on badges.
The flag of the African Natior Congress (ANC) was banned South Africa, but supporters still found ways of displaying colors. Armenia chose a new after independence (p. 57). Th SWAPO flag formed the basis independent Namibia's flag (

SOLIDARITY
This symbol incorporates both flag and people.

Rainbow symbol represents Greenpeace

FLAG OF THE "GREENS"
This is one form of the flag of Greenpeace, the international movement for protecting the earth's environment. The emblems of the dove, the olive branch, and the rainbow are all taken from the Biblical story of the flood. The green background represents the conservation of the environment and is also a symbol of hope.

Green for the environment and hope

DAY OF THE LORD
Roman Catholic festivals and processions often feature large religious banners. These examples painted with subjects such as the Virgin and Child.

THE RED FLAG
These Chinese demonstrators are carrying red flags, international symbols of socialism.

...G OF RESISTANCE
...*Union des Populations du Cameroun* was a ...stance movement in the Cameroons in the 1960s ...ch now exists only in exile. This example of their ... was captured by British troops before the ...thern Cameroons joined the Cameroon Republic.

ISLAMIC FLAG FROM THE SUDAN
This flag from the Sudan was taken by the British in 1885. It contains an inscription from the Koran (holy book of Islam), and is said to have belonged to the leader called the Mahdi.

LENIN
Many propaganda posters from the Soviet Union included the red flag.

FLAG OF HEALING
The white background of the Red Cross flag represents peace, and the cross is inspired by the cross of Switzerland (p. 33). A red crescent is used in Moslem countries.

UNITING THE NATIONS
The blue of the United Nations flag is a distinctive pale shade, now known as United Nations blue. The olive branches stand for peace and harmony.

...URCH BANNER
...the 1920s the Omega Workshop ...signed and produced many fine ...tiles, including this banner.

Flags for sports and celebrations

F LAGS ARE USED IN MANY SPORTS, including all water sports, auto races, team games, golf, gymnastics, skiing, and cross-country events. They are employed as signals, markers, team signs, supporters' favors, and decorations. They also signal the opening and closing of the events. Each Olympic Games has its own flag, and the well-known flag of the Olympic movement itself dates from 1914 and has five rings that represent the five continents that take part in the Games. When medals are presented to the victors their national anthems are played, and the opening and closing of the Games is signaled by the hoisting and lowering of the Olympic Standard.

WEAVING THEIR WAY THROUGH
Flags are used as markers in many skiing events. In slalom they define the exact path the competitor has to follow.

Sports fans encourage their heroes with and use them to show which side they suppor

LINESMEN'S FLAGS
Soccer linesmen use flags to signal to the referee when the ball has gone out of play or when players have broken the rules of the game. Flags are also used in soccer to mark the corners of the playing area.

Swivel fitting for greater flexibility

One flag in each team color

Wooden handle

Cork handle

AID TO EXERCISE
In rhythmic gymnastics, the competitors perform exercises with long streamers that are meant to be light, bright, noticeable, and graceful.

Russian rhythmic gymnast Galina Krilenko

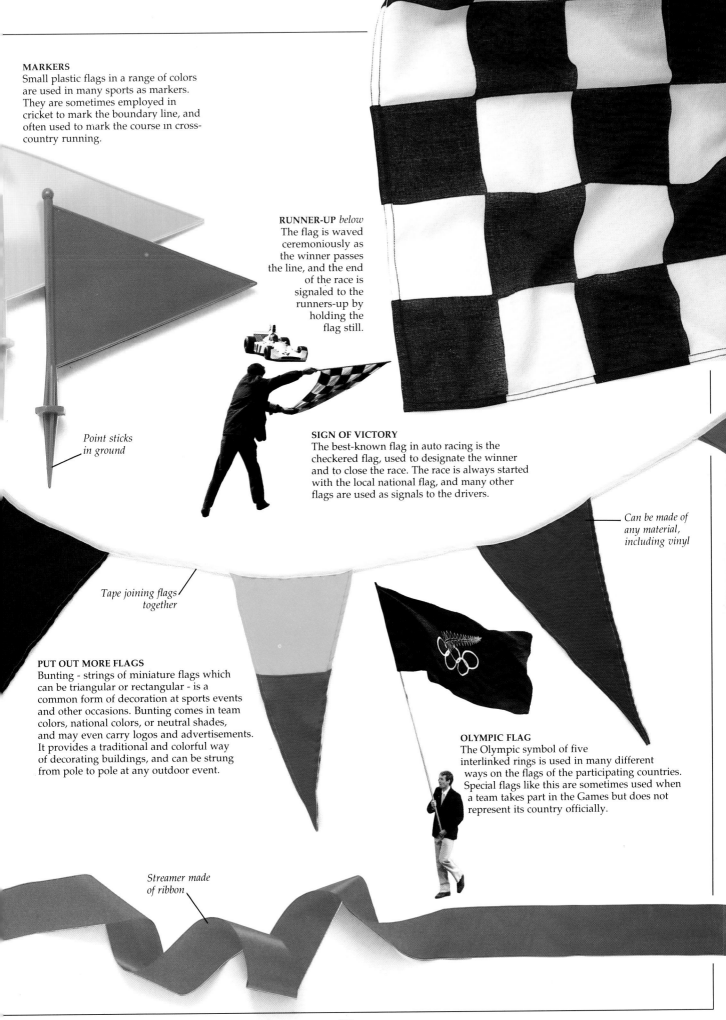

MARKERS
Small plastic flags in a range of colors are used in many sports as markers. They are sometimes employed in cricket to mark the boundary line, and often used to mark the course in cross-country running.

Point sticks in ground

RUNNER-UP *below*
The flag is waved ceremoniously as the winner passes the line, and the end of the race is signaled to the runners-up by holding the flag still.

SIGN OF VICTORY
The best-known flag in auto racing is the checkered flag, used to designate the winner and to close the race. The race is always started with the local national flag, and many other flags are used as signals to the drivers.

Can be made of any material, including vinyl

Tape joining flags together

PUT OUT MORE FLAGS
Bunting - strings of miniature flags which can be triangular or rectangular - is a common form of decoration at sports events and other occasions. Bunting comes in team colors, national colors, or neutral shades, and may even carry logos and advertisements. It provides a traditional and colorful way of decorating buildings, and can be strung from pole to pole at any outdoor event.

OLYMPIC FLAG
The Olympic symbol of five interlinked rings is used in many different ways on the flags of the participating countries. Special flags like this are sometimes used when a team takes part in the Games but does not represent its country officially.

Streamer made of ribbon

The United States of America

The STARS AND STRIPES is the best-known flag in the world, but little is known for sure about its origin. It was not designed by one person but evolved gradually. Its first form was the Cambridge (or Grand Union) Flag of the winter of 1775-76, which had thirteen stripes and the British Union Flag in the canton. In 1777 it was decided to replace the Union Flag with the blue canton and 13 stars. It is not certain exactly how the stars were first arranged - the law of 1777 refers simply to the 13 stars' representing "a new constellation" - and many different designs were made. There is a legend that Betsy Ross of Philadelphia made the first flag and presented it to George Washington, but it is more likely that Francis Hopkinson (the creator of the seal of the USA) had a hand in the design. After the Revolutionary War each star and each stripe were considered to represent a state, but later it was decided to increase only the number of stars when a new state joined the Union.

WHO WAS THE FIRST?
Robert Peary was the first man to reach the North Pole. He asserted his claim by hoisting the Stars and Stripes. His claim was disputed by Frederick Cook.

SURRENDER OF CORNWALLIS
This painting of the surrender of English general Co wallis shows the flags of the USA and of France (th Americans' ally), as they were supposed to be in 17

CAMBRIDGE FLAG
Adopted for Washington's Continental army, this flag was also called the Continental Colors.

FIRST STARS AND STRIP
This is the most familiar version of the first Stars and Stripes, although its exact form is uncertain.

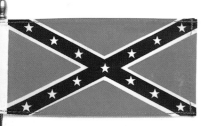

FLAG OF THE SOUTH
This flag was used in a square form in the American Civil War. The modern form is shown here.

SOUTHERN STATE
The flag of the state of Mississippi has the Southern battle flag in the canton. It was adopted after the American Civil War.

STARS AND BARS
This was the first flag of the Confederate States of America that broke away at the start of the Civil War. It flew over Fort Sumter, South Carolina, after the first shots in the war were fired there on April 12, 1861.

AMERICAN LEGION FLAG
This is the flag of a force raised from American citizens living in Canada during World War I. The flag was presented to the Legion by American-born women of Canada and is decorated with gold fringes and tassels.

STATE FLAGS
Each American state has its ow flag, as well as a coat of arms seal. This example, from Illinc is being waved at a Republica Convention at Dallas. The central device is derived fr the state seal.

50 stars - one for each of today's states.

13 stripes for the original 13 states

The specifications for the construction of the flag (size, shape, etc.) were laid down in 1912 ; those for the colors in 1934. The flag is in proportions of 10:19. Changes in the layout and number of the stars are made on the orders of the President. There are national and local laws to protect the flag from abuse.

THE STARS AND STRIPES

After the Revolutionary War it was thought that each star and stripe represented one state, and that their number had to be increased as the Union expanded. But in 1818 it was decided to increase the number of stars only, and to keep the thirteen stripes. The present form of the Stars and Stripes dates from July 4, 1960, when a fiftieth star was added for Hawaii. Changes to the flag are made on July 4 following the admission of a new state, and there have been 26 changes since 1777. Particular stars do not represent named states - it is simply the total that corresponds to the number of states in the Union.

GOOD CAUSES

The tricolor, used by some Afro-Americans, is sometimes called the Black Liberation Flag. The Christian flag, created in 1897 by Charles Overton, represents Protestants of all denominations.

SYMBOL OF A NATION *above*

The flag can be used for anything from promoting war bonds to advertising ice cream. But however it is used, it is above all a patriotic symbol for Americans all over the world. Uncle Sam is the human symbol of America, and is always shown dressed in the Stars and Stripes.

IWO JIMA

The famous photograph of marines raising the US flag on Iwo Jima (during the Pacific War in World War II) has been transformed into a memorial. The statue is an unusual instance of a real flag being combined with a piece of sculpture. The raising of the flag on Iwo Jima is a powerful symbol of the part played by the USA - and the American flag - in World War II.

FLAG ON THE MOON

One of the functions of the national flag is to symbolize conquest - including scientific and peaceful conquest.

France

SOME OF THE BEST-KNOWN flags in history come from France. The first was the *Oriflamme,* used up until the English defeated the French at the battle of Agincourt in 1451 and recognizable because of its unusual, many-tailed shape. Second were the many flags that used the traditional emblem of France, the lily (*fleur-de-lis*). Just before the revolution in 1789 the national flag was plain white, the color of the reigning Bourbon kings; the military flags were still decorated with lilies. The royal standard carried the royal arms on a background of white with gold lilies all over it. But the most famous French flag of all is the red, white, and blue flag called the *Tricolore,* used during the revolution in 1789, and familiar as a symbol of liberty throughout the world. Its colors were adopted by naval ships in 1790, with a red stripe placed at the hoist. The *Tricolore* as we know it today was introduced in 1794 and, except for a short time in the nineteenth century, has been in use ever since.

STANDARD BE
This Napol
soldier be
Tricolore, topped
one of the e
given to the regir
by the em

FOR REVOLUTION
This flag was made on board the French ship *L'Amerique* during the French Revolution. The inscription reads "Sailors, the Republic or death."

THE ROYAL LILY
Charles V of France used the *fleur-de-lis* as his emblem. Here it decorates his robes, horse's coat, and trumpeters' banners.

ROYAL RETURN
Between 1815 and 1830 the Bourbon kings of France returned to the throne. They used the simplified form of the royal arms shown on this standard.

BASTILLE DAY
Lafayette, a French general who also fought in America's Revolutionary War, took part in the celebration of the first anniversary of the fall of the Bastille. The fall of this French prison marked the start of the French Revolution.

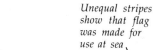

The flag is in the proportions 2:3 and is used as a national flag and a civil and naval ensign. In flags for use at sea the stripes are in the proportions 30:33:37. Each president places his personal emblem in the center to make the presidential standard.

THE *TRICOLORE*

The blue and red stripes of the *Tricolore* probably come from the colors of Paris. White is the color of the Bourbon dynasty. The red, white, and blue flag has inspired many other people to use these colors as symbols of liberty.

Unequal stripes show that flag was made for use at sea

Cross of Lorraine

GIFT OF AN EMPEROR

Napoleon awarded many flags with an eagle finial. This example was given to his Guard when he was in exile on the island of Elba. The bees were the emperor's personal emblem.

FREE FRENCH FLAG

The jack (naval flag) of the Free French ships during World War II bore the double-armed cross of Lorraine. This was the emblem of General Charles de Gaulle.

27

Germany

GERMAN EAGLE
Germany's traditional emblem, the black double-headed eagle, is seen here in a piece of stained glass showing the arms of the city of Lübeck.

GERMANY IS A COUNTRY that is very rich in flags, with two distinct rival fla traditions based on two different color combinations. Flags of both these traditions can be found in several forms. The oldest German colors are black, red, and gold, and their use on a flag dates from the time of the Napoleonic Wars (1796-1815) - before Germany was a unified country. A black, red, and gold flag was adopted by the first all-German parliament at Frankfurt in 1848, but from 1867 to 1945 a black, white, and red flag was also used. This flag was designed by the Prussian chancellor Bismarck, who

LION
This lion is from a 15th-century coat of arms.

unified the German states into a new empire in 1871. In 1919 the black-red-gold flag was again adopted, but the black, white, and red colors were eventually put back in use by Hitler in the form of the swastika flag (p. 13). Like Bismarck, Hitler took a close interest in the German flag and designed the swastika flag himself. After the defeat of the Nazis the two new states returned to the black-red-gold.

Iron Cross

Black and white colors of Prussia

Emblem of Frederick I of Prussia

FOR THE NAVY
This flag, in use between 1903 and 1921, is the *Reichskriegsflagge* or naval ensign. Based on similar previous designs, the flag features the single-headed Prussian eagle in the center. In the canton is the national flag with the Iron Cross, a Prussian emblem derived from the Teutonic knights of the Middle Ages. The large black cross was inspired by the British White Ensign.

Imperial crown

Prussian eagle

FLIGHT OF EAGLES
The eagles and coat of arms on this flag mark it as the flag of the Imperial German Crown Prince of the World War I period. It would only have been flown when the crown prince himself was present.

KISSING THE FLAG
A German soldier salutes his flag in thi patriotic picture from World War I. Suc images were often printed on postcards

28

THE "BLACK-RED-GOLD"

The black, red, and gold tricolor was adopted again in West Germany on May 8, 1949. The colors come from the uniform worn by troops of a regiment called the Lützow *Freikorps* in 1814, which was black and red with gold decorations; the flag was given the form of a tricolor a few years later. It was adopted at Frankfurt for the new united Germany of 1848. In 1919, it was re-adopted by the new German Republic, but abolished with the Nazi takeover in 1933. In 1948, it was restored in East Germany as a symbol of a re-formed country, and also subsequently in the West. Parallel versions were used in East and West Germany until 1990.

On flag arms appear in color

Arms of East Germany

THE OPPOSITION *below*
The Communist *Roter Frontkämpfer Bund* (League of Red Front Campaigners) used red flags like this during the years they were in conflict with the Nazis.

THE GATHERING STORM

The Nazis were famous for their use of flags and banners on all occasions from political rallies to army marches. The swastika appeared on the standards of the Nazi SA (*Sturm Abteilung*) together with the spread eagle and their motto, *Deutschland erwache* ("Germany awake!").

Netherlands and Belgium

THE DUTCH TRICOLOR was the first national flag in the modern sense of the word. It dates from the sixteenth century, when the Netherlands were ruled by Spain and the people were struggling against their Spanish overlords. At this time the upper stripe was orange, from the colors of William I, Prince of Orange. By 1630, however, it had changed to red, the color of the Dutch States-General, although orange still plays an important part in Dutch national heraldry. The southern provinces (the area now covered by Belgium) had broken away by 1580, and remained dependencies until 1830. This was when the kingdom of Belgium was established and the present Belgian tricolor introduced. The rampant lio is common to both countries (it is yellow on black in Belgium, red on yellow in Holland). The orange-white-blue colors of the Netherlands have been adopted in several places originally colonized by the Dutch, including New York City.

WILLIAM OF ORA
The colors of the H of Orange were use the first Dutch f

RESISTANCE BANNER
This banner was used by the Belgian Secret Army during World War II. The letters stand for the words "Secret Army" in French (*Armée Secrète*) and also in Flemish (*Geheim Leger*).

TROPHIES FROM SPAIN
The flags taken from the Spaniards by the Dutch were hung up in the Ridder-zaal in The Hague (meeting place of the States-General). Most were naval flags, and bore the red cross of Burgundy.

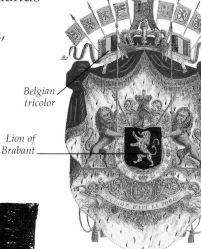

Belgian tricolor

Lion of Brabant

BELGIAN A
The gold lion on black represents region of Brabant, but also forms national arms of Belgi adopted after independenc 1830. The motto is that of States-General ("Unity is Streng Around the crest are banners of provin

FLAG FOR LIBERTY
First Belgium (1792) and then the Netherlands (1795) were taken over by the French. The Netherlands became the Batavian Republic in 1796 and adopted the Dutch tricolor with a canton showing the figure of Liberty holding the republican emblems (axes and rods, and the cap of liberty). This version was the flag used by Admiral de Winter at the Battle of Camperdown (1797), at which the British fought the French and Dutch for control of the Netherlands.

The Belgian flag being waved at a royal wedding

CITY PRIDE
All Dutch cities and towns have their own flags. The lion of Holland can be seen on the flag of Zeeland, and water-lily leaves on the flag of Friesland.

Langedijk

Zeeland

Friesland

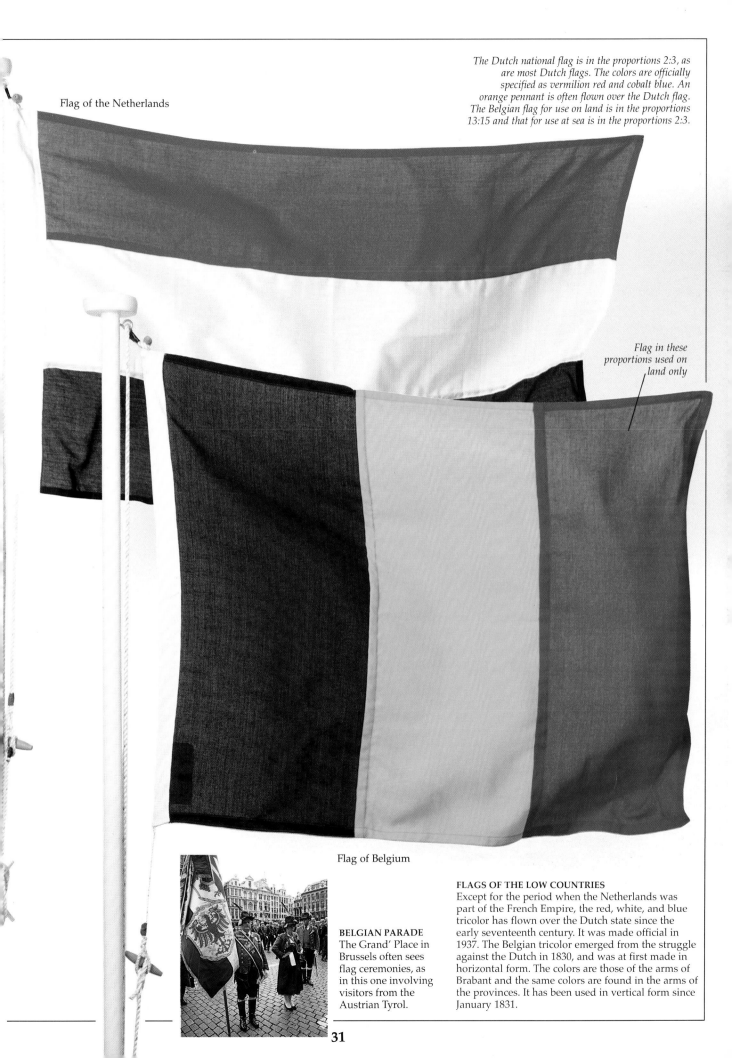

Flag of the Netherlands

The Dutch national flag is in the proportions 2:3, as are most Dutch flags. The colors are officially specified as vermilion red and cobalt blue. An orange pennant is often flown over the Dutch flag. The Belgian flag for use on land is in the proportions 13:15 and that for use at sea is in the proportions 2:3.

Flag in these proportions used on land only

Flag of Belgium

BELGIAN PARADE
The Grand' Place in Brussels often sees flag ceremonies, as in this one involving visitors from the Austrian Tyrol.

FLAGS OF THE LOW COUNTRIES
Except for the period when the Netherlands was part of the French Empire, the red, white, and blue tricolor has flown over the Dutch state since the early seventeenth century. It was made official in 1937. The Belgian tricolor emerged from the struggle against the Dutch in 1830, and was at first made in horizontal form. The colors are those of the arms of Brabant and the same colors are found in the arms of the provinces. It has been used in vertical form since January 1831.

Austria and Switzerland

THE ORIGINAL REGIONS (or "cantons") of Switzerland were ruled by Austria dukes until the fourteenth century, when the regions threw off Austrian ru and formed a loose confederation which was joined by other Swiss states The emblem that they chose derives from the symbol of the central cant of Schwyz. It was adopted by the other cantons as a battle flag in 1339 a as a common banner in 1480, but it was not widely used as a nationa flag until after 1848. Austria, meanwhile, grew into a large empire, which lasted until 1918. Th red and white colors of the Austrian flag come from the arms of the dukes who were in power at the time of the struggle with Switzerland; th colors have been used in this form since at leas 1230. Both Austria and Switzerland have strong heraldic traditions along German lines (pp. 28-29) and every region has its own arm and flag. Many of the Swiss regional flags contain heraldic emblems; the majority of the Austrian flags are plainer striped designs.

This figure carries a flag in the Imperial colors of Austria.

FLAG OF AN EMPIRE
From 1867 to 1918 Austria and Hungary were ruled by the same emperor. The Austro-Hungarian empire used this flag at sea, which combines both their colors and shields.

LOCAL BANNERS
Most cantons of Switzerland use their armorial banners as local flags. They have the same designs as their coats of arms. The flag of Bern has the image of a bear, which can be seen all over the city. The flag of Uri portrays a wild ox, after which the canton is named. That of Lucerne uses the same colors as the local arms, but these are arranged in horizontal bands rather than the vertical ones of the shield.

Bern

Lucerne

PROUD AND PROMINENT
There is a famous display of flags on the Pont de Mont Blanc, Geneva. Visible are those of the Swiss cantons Thurgau, Bern, Fribourg, Glarus, and Graubünden.

Uri

NATIONAL HERO
Arnold von Winkelried is a legendary Swiss hero who is supposed to have helped his country to victory over Austria. By seizing as many enemy spears as he could reach and creating a gap in the Austrian lines, he was able to give the Swiss the advantage in the Battle of Sempach (1386).

HERALDIC BEASTS
Many Swiss coats of arms are based on animals, like this goat in a stained-glass window at the castle of Chillon.

ON GUARD
The Swiss Guards at the Vatican in Rome have a distinctive colored uniform.

The flag of Austria is in proportions of 2:3. The form used by private citizens is shown here - for official purposes the coat of arms is placed in the center. The Swiss flag is square, but a civil ensign in proportions of 2:3 was introduced in 1941.

Flag of Austria

Flag of Switzerland

FOLLOW THE BEAR
This large statue of a bear in the city of Bern is one example of the local emblem.

NATIONAL FLAGS
The flag of Austria is one of the oldest national flags in the world. One legend says that the design was based on the bloodstained tunic of Duke Leopold V - the only part of the tunic that remained white was the area under his broad belt. The flag of Switzerland, on the other hand, was only adopted officially in 1848.

Italy

BEFORE 1861, Italy was a collection of many separate states, some ruled by foreign dynasties, others under the control of the Cathol Church. Each state had its own flag and heraldry, and there was no attempt at unity until the end of the eighteenth century. The colors of Italy were established during the great wave of activity when Napoleon invaded Italy in 1796. They were influenced by the French *Tricolore* (pp. 26-27) and were at first used in a horizontal form. The vertical tricolor was introduced in 1798, but was only used until the fall of Napoleon, with whom the flag was so closely associated, in 1802. In 1848, "The Year of Revolutions," the tricolor appeared again in the Italian states. The form adopted by Sardinia eventually became the flag of the new Kingdom of Italy, which was formed in 1861 after Garibaldi united Italy in the movement known as the *Risorgimento* (resurgence). The kingdom lasted until 1946, when the arms were removed from the flag, which is now a plain tricolor of green, white, and red.

HERO OF THE
RISORGIMENTO
Garibaldi and his Red Shirts started the movement to unite Italy in 1860.

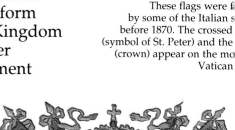

Rome   Papal Sta

Naples

KEY
ST. P
These flags were f
by some of the Italian s
before 1870. The crossed
(symbol of St. Peter) and the
(crown) appear on the mo
Vatican

GLORY
IN BATTLE
Italian soldiers carried the Sardinian version of the tricolor at the battle of Ain-Zara in 1911.

Blue-bordered arms of Savoy

SYMBOLS OF UNITY
The shield and crown of Savoy, combined with Italian flags, formed a popular patriotic symbol.

CAPTURED IN AFRICA
This Italian national flag flew over the fortre of Gondar, Ethiopia, after Italy took over in It was captured when the Ethiopian empero reconquered his country, with the help of th British, in 1941.

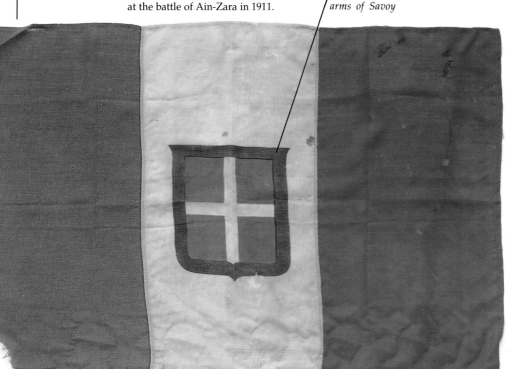

THE LION OF ST. MARK
The ancient flag of Venice bore the lion, and a lion flag still flie in St. Mark's Square today.

Green was said to be Napoleon's favorite color

Blank central area shows this is the Italian flag, not the flag of Mexico

The flag is in proportions of 2:3, with three equal stripes

THE ITALIAN TRICOLOR

The colors of the Italian flag have been said to represent the virtues of Faith, Hope, and Charity, but they are in fact inspired by the French *Tricolore*. They also incorporate the green and white colors of the Milanese militia. There are several variations: the flags used at sea have shields in the center to set them apart from the flag of Mexico (p. 60); the naval ensign also has a naval crown above the shield.

SYMBOL OF THE LEFT

The Italian colors are combined with the hammer and sickle to form the symbol of the Communist Party of Italy.

GROUP OF ALLIES

The British, French, and Italians were allies during World War I. This propaganda picture shows their soldiers and their flags, with the caption "All against the Germans." The Red Ensign (p. 16), and not the Union Jack, has been used to represent Britain, a common mistake at this time.

RACE FOR THE FLAG

Twice a year in Sienna the colorful spectacle of the *Palio* horse race can be seen. The participants represent the seventeen districts of the city, who compete for the honor of displaying the *Palio* (an ancient flag bearing an image of the Virgin Mary) in their local church. They carry brightly colored square flags like this.

This lapel badge shows the modern Spanish flag.

Spain and Portugal

ALTHOUGH THEY LOOK VERY DIFFERENT, the flags of Spain and Portugal share a simple two-color design to which different coats of arms have been added. Yellow and red, the colors of Spain, were adopted as recently as 1785, but they have a longer history as the traditional colors of the regions of Castile and Aragon. The yellow and red flag was first created during the French Revolution (p. 26). Since then, there has always been a coat of arms on the state flag and ensign. First the arms of Castile and Leon were used, but while Francisco Franco was dictator (1939-47), they were replaced by the national arms. When the monarchy was restored, the present arms were added, but no arms appear on flags for civil use. Portugal adopted a distinctive blue and white flag in 1830. These colors were also traditional, but in 1910 Portugal became a republic, and the colors were changed to red and green.

EARLY COLONY
An old form of the Portuguese flag is shown on this map of the Guinea coast (c. 1502). The blue shields and white disks were known as the *quinas*, and the yellow castles on red were called the bordure of Castile.

AT SEA
The Spanish colors can be seen in this painting of the Armada (1588).

IN ACTIVE SERVICE
The 1785 version of the Spanish naval ensign is red and yellow with the crowned arms of Castile and Leon. The arms are usually set toward the hoist, so this example has probably lost some material at the fly end while being used.

OLD AND NEW
The 1830 flag of Portugal (left) is strikingly different from the modern flag, but the blue shields still appear. The modern flag of the Azores (right) i adapted from the 1830 flag of Port The Azores flag bears a hawk (*açor* Portuguese).

SPANISH FLAG?
The red and yellow flag in this picture is not a Spanish flag - simply the international signal flag for the letter Y.

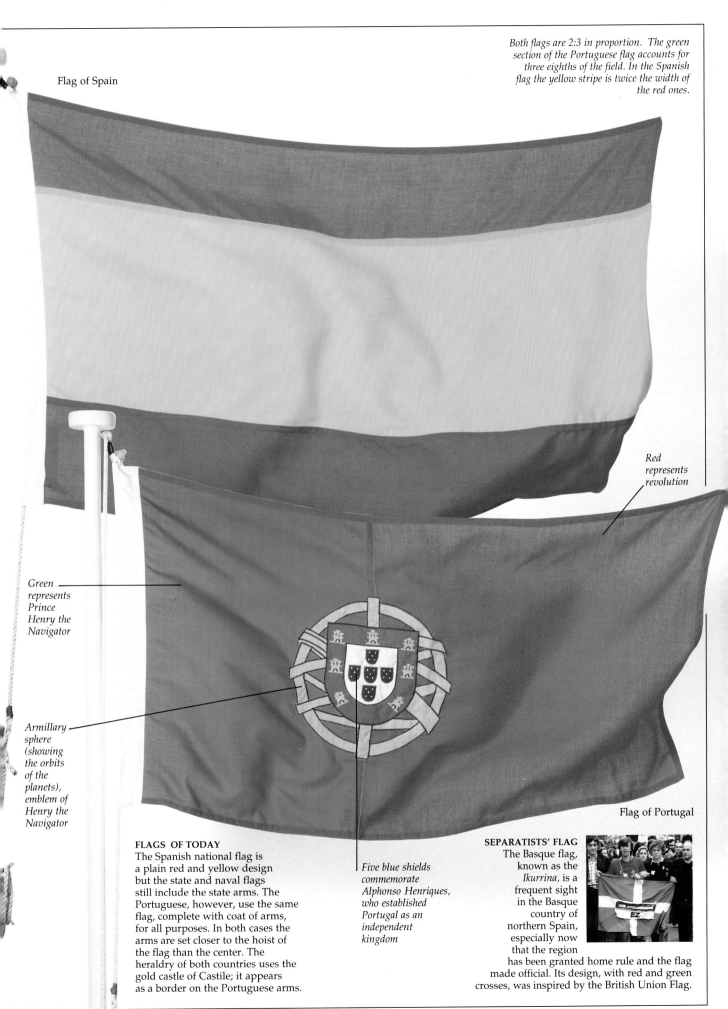

Flag of Spain

Red
represents
revolution

Green
represents
Prince
Henry the
Navigator

Armillary
sphere
(showing
the orbits
of the
planets),
emblem of
Henry the
Navigator

Flag of Portugal

FLAGS OF TODAY
The Spanish national flag is
a plain red and yellow design
but the state and naval flags
still include the state arms. The
Portuguese, however, use the same
flag, complete with coat of arms,
for all purposes. In both cases the
arms are set closer to the hoist of
the flag than the center. The
heraldry of both countries uses the
gold castle of Castile; it appears
as a border on the Portuguese arms.

Five blue shields
commemorate
Alphonso Henriques,
who established
Portugal as an
independent
kingdom

SEPARATISTS' FLAG
The Basque flag,
known as the
Ikurrina, is a
frequent sight
in the Basque
country of
northern Spain,
especially now
that the region
has been granted home rule and the flag
made official. Its design, with red and green
crosses, was inspired by the British Union Flag.

Greece and Balkan

IN THE NINETEENTH CENTURY, these two Christian countries struggled to free themselves from the rule of the Moslem Turks. Their flags reflect the struggle in different ways. Greece based its symbolism on the cross and Christian banners. The blue and white in the Greek flag come from an early flag, and from the colors of Bavaria – a prince of that country became the first king of Greece in 1832. The stripes are thought to represent the syllables of the Greek motto (translated as "Liberty or death"). Whether or not this is true, it shows how closely the flag is linked to the movement for freedom. When Serbia fought for independence in 1912, they used the red, white and blue of Russia, the country which helped them in their victory. These colors became known as the "Slav" colours. When the Federal Socialist Republic of Yugoslavia formed, the red star of Communism was added to the flag. Four of the former Yugoslav republics became independent states in 1992.

This figure represents the 19th-century idea of Greek elegance and beauty.

FLAGS FOR FREEDOM
In 1992, the Yugoslav republics regained their independence. In Croatia, the ancient arms of red and white were revived.

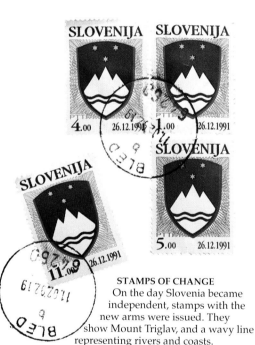

STAMPS OF CHANGE
On the day Slovenia became independent, stamps with the new arms were issued. They show Mount Triglav, and a wavy line representing rivers and coasts.

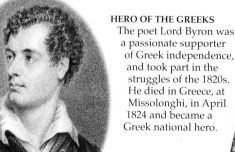

SYMBOL OF DIVIS
The Croatian flag is ho' to indicate the new st frontier. The disputes the division of Yugos' led to the bloodiest w Europe since World W.

Greek colors at the Royal Palace, Athens

HERO OF THE GREEKS
The poet Lord Byron was a passionate supporter of Greek independence, and took part in the struggles of the 1820s. He died in Greece, at Missolonghi, in April 1824 and became a Greek national hero.

EARLY GREEK FLAG
This Greek postage stamp shows an early Greek national flag. The traditional Greek colors have a long history of use.

The Greek flag is in proportions of 7:12.
The blue of the flag has varied over the
years. It is now a bright intermediate shade.
The proportions of the Yugoslav flag
are 1:2, but the commercial flag is 2:3.

Cross recalls
religious origins
of the freedom
movement

Flag of Greece

Flag of Yugoslavia (Serbia
and Montenegro)

Flag no longer has a red
star emblem in the center

NATIONAL FLAGS
The design of the Greek flag is inspired by the
American Stars and Stripes, but incorporates the
Christian symbol of the cross. The layout of the
stripes in the Yugoslav flag dates from 1918,
when Serbia and the other Yugoslav states
formed a united kingdom. Until the time of the
German occupation, the national flag consisted
of a plain tricolor. Tito placed the red star in the
center at the start of Communist rule, and the
flags of the constituent republics also acquired
red stars. Following the breakup of the federation
in 1992, two states, Serbia and Montenegro, kept
the name Yugoslavia and kept the flag, but
removed the Communist red star.

MEETING OF ALLIES
This picture of a
demonstration in Salonika
during 1916 shows the Greek
flag, together with those of
Italy, France, the
Netherlands, and the
British Red Ensign.

Denmark

The Danish flag on a 19th-century Christmas card.

THE DANES HAVE one of the oldest flags still in use, and there are two different stories of its origin. According to legend, the red flag with a white cross fell from heaven in 1219 during a battle at which the Christian Danes were victorious over the pagan Estonians. But according to historical records, the flag first appeared in the arms of King Valdemar Atterdag in the fourteenth century. At that time the cross had arms of equal length, like the cross of St. George (p. 46), but over the years the outer arm lengthened to produce the characteristic Scandinavian cross. As with the English flag of St. George, the colors of the cross are not those of the royal arms (the red and white flag was in general use in Christian Europe). The Danish cross and flag form spread to other Scandinavian countries and to Finland and Germany; it can also be found in Normandy, a memento of the days when Norsemen colonized Europe. The Danes themselves are great flag-flyers, and the Danish flag can be seen in a variety of settings in Denmark - from government buildings and town halls to back gardens and Christmas trees.

EARLY ORIGINS
The Danish flag first appeared on the arms of King Valdemar IV Atter (1340-75). The royal shie the same today.

SPLITFLAG
This early 15th-century seal sh the swallowtail version of the Danish flag, call the splitflag. It is used for naval and official purposes.

Dragoon standard from the reign of Christian IV (1588-1648).

Musketeer company flag from the reign of Christian VII (1766-1808) used in the Napoleonic Wars.

Infantry flag from the reign of Christian IV (1588-1648).

TERROR INHOSTES

ARMY FLAGS
Denmark has a strong tradition of military flags. Many include the Danish cross. The infantry flag has the national flag in the canton, and the device of a chain-mailed fist emerging from a cloud, dealing out thunderbolts. The motto is "Terror to the enemy." The Musketeer flag also uses the Danish cross; the Dragoon flag carries a classical image of victory.

FLAG OF THE FAEROES
The Faeroe Islands have had their own flag since 1931, with a design based on the flags of Denmark and Iceland. The flag became official, for use on land only, in 1948.

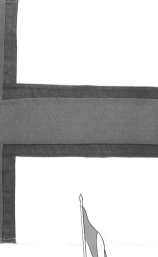

MODE COLOR
Flags o military of today generally on the D nation flag.

40

Inner cantons are three sevenths of width

The flag is in proportions of 28:37, which were laid down in 1848. The naval flag is somewhat longer (56:107). The width of the cross is one seventh of the width of the flag. For official purposes badges are often placed in the canton, or in the center of the cross.

THE DANNEBROG
The Danish flag is known as the Dannebrog, or "Danish cloth." Although it is a very old design, its precise proportions were only laid down in 1848. Its design has given rise to the flags of Norway, Iceland, the Faeroe Islands, and probably also to those of Sweden and Finland. But the exact proportions of the flag and the cross are unlike those of any other country.

FLYING THE FLAG
The Danes are proud of the Dannebrog and display it everywhere. It even appears in peoples' private backyards (left) and is sometimes used by the young as a pattern for makeup (above).

Beer can illustration showing Danish flags flying over cottages

IN THE POLAR WASTES
Greenland, a part of Denmark that has home rule, acquired its own flag for use on land and at sea in 1985. The design was the winning entry in a competition. It is in the Danish colors, and it represents the sun rising over the polar ice.

Norway and Iceland

THE FLAGS of Norway and Iceland are very similar. They have a common origin - both designs are based on that of the flag of Denmark, the country to which both once belonged.

The flag of Norway was designed in 1821 after control of the country had passed to Sweden. The blue cross was added so that the colors were the same as those of the French tricolor. In the nineteenth century there was a struggle to get this flag accepted for use at sea and on land without any "union" markings symbolizing Norway's link with Sweden. This was only achieved in 1899 and le to the dissolving of the union with Sweden in 1905. In the Icelandic flag the blue and white are said to come from the colors of the Order of the Silver Falcon. The flag was created in 1913, and was allowed to be used at sea after 1918, when Iceland became a separate realm of the Danish crown. When the island became an independent republic in 1944, the flag became the national flag.

SCANDINAVIAN CROSS
The arms of Denmark show the cross, which influenced the design of both the Norwegian and Icelandic flags.

SUPERB STANDARD
This ornate flag is a cavalry standard made in the city of Trondheim in the late seventeenth century. It is richly embroidered on a red damask fabric. Its shape recalls some of the European military guidons (pp. 12–13), which are also elaborately decorated.

Cavalry standard

ENEMY AT THE GATES
Both these Norwegian flags a cavalry standard and a regimental color - date from the 17th century. Each one bears the arms of Norway, a lion holding a long-handled ax. In the corner of the caval standard is the cross of Denmark, to which Norway belonged until 1814. The regimental color is that of Hannibal Sehested's regime and bears his motto, "Hann is at the gates."

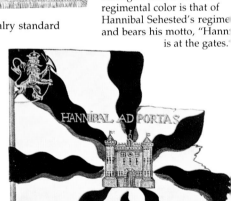

Cavalry standard

Regimental color

CONQUERING THE POLE
The Norwegian flag is notable for being the first at the South Pole, which was reached by Captain Roald Amundsen on December 14, 1911. It took Amundsen and his four companions 55 days to reach the Pole, using skis and sleds pulled by dogs to transport their supplies. They left the Norwegian flag in the ice and it was still there when Captain Scott, Amundsen's British rival, reached the South Pole a month later.

SWALLOWTAIL
The naval ensign of Iceland takes a distinctive swallow-tailed form. The custom of using this shape for naval and official purposes is common in Scandinavia.

The flag of Norway is made in proportions of 8:11. The proportions of the Icelandic flag are 18:25. The inner cantons of the Norwegian flag are half the length of the outer ones.

Narrow inner canton

Fimbriation

Flag of Norway

Fimbriation

Flag of Iceland

NATIONAL FLAGS
In the flag of Norway the cross and its surrounding fimbriation (border) are one quarter the width of the flag, whereas in the Icelandic flag they are wider. Both countries use swallow-tailed versions of their flags, but those of Norway have an extension of the cross as well, forming a tongue, as used in Sweden and Finland. Badges can be placed in the canton or in the center of the cross.

Sweden and Finland

SWEDISH ARMS
Flags and heraldry have a long history in Sweden. The three crowns of the medieval state arms are shown here. This Swedish soldier also carries a very long lance-pennon (p. 6).

FINLAND WAS PART OF SWEDEN from the twelfth century until 1809, but never lost its individual character. In 1809 it became part of the Russian Empire and in 1917 finally achieved independence, joining the Scandinavian group of nations. Both Sweden and Finland have national flags based on the Scandinavian cross. In the case of Sweden the colors come from the traditional arms, and in Finland they are based on the blue a white used in the nineteenth century to represent the blue lakes and white snows of the country. The Swedish cross on a flag dates back to at least 1533; the arms with their gold crowns on a blue background date back to 1364. As in Denmark, flags form an important part of Swedish life, and a national flag day is celebrated on June 6 each year. Finland's arms were granted by King John of Sweden in 1581. They include a lion treading on a scimitar (a common Moslem symbol), representing victory over enemies from the East, and nine roses, which stand for the country's nine provinces.

A Swe
knig.
the 14th cen
covered
her
emb

GUSTAVUS VASA
King Gustav I of Sweden reigned from 1523 to 1560 and was a member of the House of Vasa. He fought for Sweden against the Danes, whom he defeated in 1523. He is remembered as a just and pious king.

SCANIA
This region in southern Sweden is trying to secure home rule; its flag is well known in Sweden. Scania was ruled by Denmark until 1658, and the colors of the flag come from those of Denmark and Sweden.

ALAND ISLANDS
This flag dates from the 1920s and represents a group of islands that belong to Finland but are inhabited mainly by Swedes. The colors combine the blue and yellow of Sweden with the red and yellow of the islands' arms.

The traditio
arms of Swed
on a milit
stand

Flag of Sweden

The flags of the Scandinavian countries are all slightly different in their proportions and in the proportions of their crosses. Sweden's flag is made in proportions of 5:8, and the width of the cross is 20 percent of the overall width of the flag. The flag of Finland is in proportions of 11:18 and the cross is three elevenths of the width. The state flag of Finland bears the arms in the center of the cross.

Flag of Finland

NATIONAL FLAGS

During the union with Norway (1814-1905), the flag of Sweden had a "union mark" in the canton. Modern flags date from the Flag Law of 1906. The flag of Finland evolved in the nineteenth century, but was only chosen officially in 1918. The blue and white colors first appeared in 1860, and various designs were suggested before the Scandinavian cross proved triumphant.

NAVAL VERSION

The Swedes use this shape of flag for ships. The Swedish royal flag has a similar shape with the royal arms in the center.

FINNISH ARMS

This postage stamp shows the coat of arms of Finland, with the lion treading on a scimitar and nine roses.

SUOMI FINLAND 10,00

The United Kingdom

SINCE THE THIRTEENTH CENTURY, the English have flown a flag bearing the red cross of St. George, the country's patron saint. This was the flag behind which they rode into battle on the crusades against the Moslems (12th and 13th centuries), although they also carried flags bearing the English royal arms. At about the same time the Scottish adopted as their flag the saltire cross of St. Andrew, a white cross on a blue background. After the two kingdoms were united in 1603, these two crosses were combined to produce one of the most striking flag designs - the Union Flag. When Ireland came under direct British rule in 1800, the red cross of St. Patrick was incorporated into the design to produce the flag we know today. The fourth country of the United Kingdom, Wales, is not represented in the Union Flag; the Welsh have their own flag, which bears a red dragon on a white and green field.

ROYAL FUNE
The banners of Engl. Ireland, Wales, Chester, Cornwall decorated the fur train of Queen Elizab in 1

DEATH IN BATTLE
This painting of the death of Major Pierson at the Battle of St. Helier, Jersey, shows the pre-1801 version of the Union Flag. The British were fighting the French for control of the Channel Islands.

Plain white diagonals show that this flag was made before 1801. Badly aligned diagonals are a common mistake in flag-making; this flag was probably made aboard ship

SAVING THE COLORS
These British Guards are saving their colors at the Battle of Inkerman in the Crimean War (1853-56). Troops made every effort to keep their flags from being captured.

EARLY VERSION
Lord Howe's command flag was flown on his ship HMS *Queen Charlotte* at the Battle of the First of June, 1794, during the French Revolutionary Wars.

Red hand is the traditional emblem of Ulster

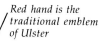

CARRYING THE COLORS
The "ensign" was t most junior officer regiment. He carrie the colors, and too his title from them. This 19th-century painting shows an ensign of the 75th Highlanders Regiment.

This flag, based on the Ulster coat of arms, was used from 1953 until the British imposed direct rule of Northern Ireland in 1972.

Although the union with Ireland was dissolved in 1921, St. Patrick's cross still remains in the flag

There are no official specifications for the construction of the flag. It is usually made in proportions of 1:2, but the colors can be any shade of red and blue.

White diagonals
for Scotland

Blue background
for Scotland

White background
for England

England

Scotland

Ireland

THREE FLAGS IN ONE
The English cross of St. George and the Scottish saltire are still very widely used, although the cross of St. Patrick has been largely replaced by the flags of Ulster (see opposite) and Eire (p. 61).

THE "UNION JACK"
Although its correct name is the Union Flag, the British national flag is usually known as the Union Jack. A jack is any small flag flown from the jackstaff at the bow of a ship; the Union Jack is used in this way only by the Queen. It is flown on the mainmast by the Admiral of the Fleet. The Union Jack is the national flag for use on land. It is also used by the Commander in Chief of the British army.

FLAG AS FASHION
In the 1960s the Union Jack was used on clothes and other items.

FLAG FOR HIGH FLIERS
This special ensign was produced for the Royal Air Force at the time of the Armistice celebrations at the end of World War I in 1918. The modern RAF ensign was introduced some two years later.

BRITISH BULLDOG
During the Boer War and World War I the Union Jack was used widely as a patriotic symbol.

Canada and New Zealand

ARMS OF NEW ZEALAND
The arms have the Southern Cross in the main quarter. The royal crown replaced the previous crest in 1953.
The "supporters" carry a New Zealand flag and a Maori spear. Around the scroll are leaves of fern, the national badge.

CANADA WAS THE FIRST DOMINION to be set up within the British Empire, but the last to adopt a distinctive flag. New Zealand, on the other hand, had its own local ensign even before it became part of the empire. Under British influence, Maori chiefs chose the "Waitangi" flag in 1834 and used it until 1840, when they handed over control of New Zealand to Queen Victoria. After this, New Zealand used British ensigns with various badges, until the four stars of the Southern Cross (pp. 50-51) were adopted in 1896. The form of the Southern Cross used in New Zealand is similar to that on the Australian flag, but has only four stars. They were originally red on a white disk and when the red stars were placed on the fly of the Blue Ensign, they were outlined in white so that they could be seen more clearly. Canada also used British ensigns after it became a federal dominion in 1867. In 1892 the use of a shield of arms on the Red Ensign was authorized for use at sea, and after 1945 this became the form used on land as well. In 1965 the present design was introduced, using the maple leaf, which had been an emblem of Canada since the nineteenth century. It was only adopted after the longest parliamentary debate in Canadian history. The provinces of Canada also developed ensign badges. Newfoundland did the same, and had its own set of ensigns before 1949, when it became part of Canada.

Bicentennial badge from the province of Ontario, Canada (1784-1984)

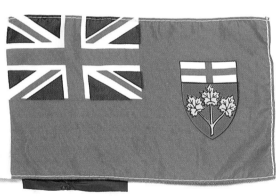

BRITISH BANNER
A British Red Ensign with the provincial shield in the fly makes up the flag of Ontario. The shield, with its yellow maple leaves, dates from 1868, and the flag was made official in 1965. It emphasizes the British link with Canada.

BRITISH LINKS
The Red Ensign with Canadian shield was used by Canada in both world wars. The Canadian state arms still include the Union Jack

FOR THE FRENCH
Known as the *fleurdelysé* flag, the banner of Québec comes from an earlier 19th-century version, and represents French-speakers throughout Canada. The *fleur-de-lis* and the white cross on blue recall the flags of pre-revolutionary France (p. 26).

SUN IN SPLENDOR
The device of the setting sun on the British Columbian banner refers to the province's geographical position as the westernmost state, and also to the motto on its arms: *Splendor sine Occasu* ("A splendor that never sets").

Flag of Canada

Canada's most popular emblem, the leaf of the local tree, the red maple

Red and white are the heraldic colors of Canada and the square white panel in the flag is known in heraldry as the Canadian pale. The flag, in proportions of 1:2, was officially adopted in 1965.

Flag of New Zealand

Stars outlined in white so that they stand out clearly

NATIONAL FLAGS
The Blue Ensign of New Zealand was officially adopted for use at sea and on land in 1902, although Maoris use the Red Ensign on land, since red is their traditional color. With the adoption of the distinctive Canadian flag in 1965, Australia, New Zealand, Fiji, and Tuvalu are the only countries of the British Commonwealth whose flags still include the Union Jack. The flag of Canada includes the leaf of the maple, a familiar tree in Canada and a Canadian symbol with a long history. The flag may be used both at sea and on land.

HANDING OVER
The Treaty of Waitangi (1840) turned the Maoris into British subjects.

Australia

THE SOUTHERN CROSS, a bright constellation visible from the Southern Hemisphere that has been used for centuries by sailo as a navigational aid, has been a major theme in Australian symbolism since the early nineteenth century. The first flag to carry the four stars of the Southern Cross was the National Colonial Flag of 1823-24, which placed them on the red cross of t British White Ensign. In 1831 the New South Wales ensign appeared, very similar to the Commonwealth flag (see below), but with stars of eight points. In due course this became the "Federation" flag. In 1854 the Eureka Stockade flag appeared, an there were several other adaptations of the emblem, including th ensign badge of Victoria (1870). So it is not surprising that the Southern Cross figured in the design which won the competition for a flag after Australia became a federal dominion in 1901. The resulting flag consisted of the Southern Cross on a blue field with the Union Jack in the canton. The stars are not quite the same as those in the flag of Victoria, and their varying numbers of points indicate the brilliance of the actual stars. The flag also had a large star of six points, standing for the six states. This was changed to a seven-pointed star in 1908, so that the Northern Territory of Australia was also represented.

DISCOVERER OF TASMANIA
In 1642 Abel Tasman discovered the island that now bears his name (it was formerly Van Diemen's Land). He was exploring on behalf of the Dutch East India Company and his ship carried their tricolor flag.

THE EUREKA FLAG
This flag originally represented th Ballarat Reform League of 1854, which represented the gold miner who were fighting for a fairer licensing system for mining and for electoral reforms. It was hoisted over the stockade where t miners resisted the state troopers. Although the protest was quickly put down by the soldiers, a reform league was established to examine disputes between the m and the government. The reputa of the Eureka Stockade as a focus radical ideas has lived on, and t flag is still popular in Australia, particularly as a republican sym

Stars could have five or eight points

Design comes from flag of New South Wales (1831)

FLAG FOR UNITY
The Federation flag stood for the idea of uniting the six Australian states as an independent nation, which was not achieved until January 1, 1901. During the last two decades of the 19th century the Australian Natives Association and the Australian Federation League popularized the idea by displaying this flag.

BOUNCING BACK
One of these boomerangs is decorated with designs from t Australian flag.

Union Jack signifies the link with Britain and the Commonwealth

Commonwealth Star

Crux Australis
(the Southern Cross)

WINNING DESIGN

A total of 32,823 designs were entered for the competition to find a flag for Australia in 1900. Five separate entrants submitted the winning design, which was officially adopted in February 1903 for use on Australian vessels and became the legal national flag in April 1954. The flag design consists of three parts: the Union Flag (showing the link with Britain), the Southern Cross (for Australia), and the Commonwealth Star (for the federal system). The official national colors of Australia, however, are green and yellow, and many of the new proposals for Australian flags use these colors.

New South Wales

Queensland

Western Australia

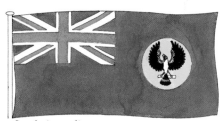

South Australia

Tasmania

Victoria

ABORIGINAL LAND RIGHTS FLAG

This flag has become a powerful symbol for the native people of Australia. Black represents the people, the yellow circle stands for the sun, and the red is for the land of Australia.

STATE FLAGS

Each of Australia's six states has a flag, based on the British Blue Ensign, with the relevant badge in the fly. The badges are patterned after the states' coats of arms. Recently South Australia changed its arms to the same design as the flag-badge. Each state governor also has a flag. The flags date from the following years: 1875 (Tasmania, Western Australia), 1876 (New South Wales, Queensland), 1877 (Victoria), and 1904 (South Australia). The Northern Territory also has its own flag.

Japan

THE NAME JAPAN means "source of the sun." This fact is clearly reflecte[d] in Japanese flag design, for the two best-known forms of the Japanese flag are the red sun-disk on a white field (the national flag of today), and the Rising Sun which has red rays extending from the sun to the edge of the flag. For centuries, Japan was virtually a "closed" country, avoiding all foreign influence and doing without a national flag. However, the sun-disk design is an old one, and was revived after the visit of the American commodore Matthew Perry in 1853, when Japan finally opened its doors to the influence of the West. The sun-disk was first used as a national ensign, then legalized on February 27, 1870, following the Meiji Restoration of 1868, when the military commander (shogun) was overthrown and the emperor reclaimed his political power. The flag's name in Japanese is *Hinomaru*, the sun-disk flag.

A 19th-century Western view of a Japanese woman.

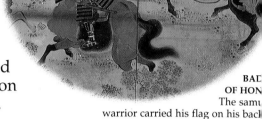

BA[D]
OF HON[OR]
The sam[urai]
warrior carried his flag on his bac[k]
usually bore his family heraldic emblem, or m[on]

FLAG WITH PHOENIXES
Captured from the Japanese by the British in 1945, this flag includes two phoenixes surrounding a heraldic emblem, or *mon*. In Eastern thought the phoenix symbolizes the sun. This device can be seen today on the flag of the president of South Korea.

THE RISING SUN
This flag was adopted as the naval and military ensign on November 3, 1889, but was outlawed at the end of World War II. However, it was revived for the Maritime Defense Force in June 1954 and forms the basis for the rank flags of admirals. A flag with the same basic design is used today for the Ground Self-Defense Force. This example is from World War II.

*Proportions 1:2
(modern version is 2:3)*

VICTORY!
The Rising Sun ensign flew on the Japanese ships at the Battle of Tsushima, 1905, when the Japanese defeated a Russian fleet.

Phoenix represents the sun

The color of the red of the disk is kurenai, or vermilion

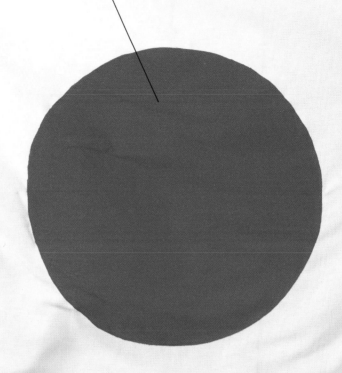

THE SUN-DISK FLAG
One of the simplest national flags, the sun-disk was first hoisted at sea in 1855, carried to America in 1860, and made the basis of regimental colors in 1870. It was approved for private use in 1872. The white ground is said to stand for purity and integrity and the red disk for sincerity, brightness, and warmth, and so the flag symbolizes the Japanese ideal of *Akaki kiyoki tadashiki naoki makoto no kokoro* ("Bright, pure, just, and of gentle heart").

Inscription radiates from center of flag

SOLDIER'S PRAYERS
During World War II soldiers carried flags inscribed with prayers, often made for them by their families. The prayers were never written on the sun-disk itself. Many such flags ended up as souvenirs in enemy hands.

IN HONOR OF THE EMPEROR
Flags are often used on feast days and holidays. In fact the Japanese sign for a holiday is two crossed flags. Here the flag is used to greet the emperor, who has his own personal flag bearing the chrysanthemum *mon* in gold on red.

Africa and South America

THE FLAGS OF THESE CONTINENTS have emerged from periods of revolution and freedom from bondage. The peoples of Latin America began to throw off the rule of Spain in the early years of the nineteenth century, with the help of soldiers like Miranda of Venezuela, Bolívar of Bolivia, and San Martín of Argentina. Not surprisingly, many of their flags were tricolors, inspired by the French flag but using colors associated with the Latin American national heroes. Many of these tricolors still form the basis of the national flags of Latin America. In Africa the process of gaining independence was the work of lawyers and politicians such as Nkrumah of Ghana and Kenyatta of Kenya. In designing their flags, the people of the new African nations looked to the example of Ethiopia, a country that had avoided foreign rule for many years. The Ethiopian flag of green, yellow, and red had been adopted by the West Indians and combined with the colors of black liberation (p. 25) to make the well-known Rastafarian combination. Ghana became the first African state adopt these colors, in 1957; since then they have become widespread.

BIRDS OF A FEATHER
Mexico makes use of Aztec traditions in its arms, which depict the legend of the foundation of Mexico City. These arms appear on the tricolor flag of Mexico.

ALL CHANGE
A new country, a new stamp, a new flag. Gambia's flag was adopted in 1965.

FLAG OF CONFLICT
This marker flag was used by the King's African Rifles during the British campaign against the Mau Mau movement in Kenya. This 1950s movement aimed to gain better conditions for Africans under British rule, and the struggles between the two sides led eventually to independence from Britain in 1963. The figure 3 in the flag stands for the 3rd platoon. The flag's crude manufacture suggests that it was locally made.

IN THE VANGUARD
The Ethiopian flag flew at the Battle of Lasta during the war of 1896.

RASTAFARIAN COLORS
The flag of Ethiopia emerged in the 1890s. It was the inspiration the Rastafarians, a West Indian cult whose members reject Western culture and ideas and regard Haile Selassie, the former Ethiopian emperor, as divine. Ethiopia remained free of colonization until 1936 and was admired for its resistance.

PRIDE OF KENYA
Peter Rono, Olympic gold medal winner at Seoul in 1988, carries the flag of Kenya. It is based on the colors admired by Jomo Kenyatta, the father of modern Kenya.

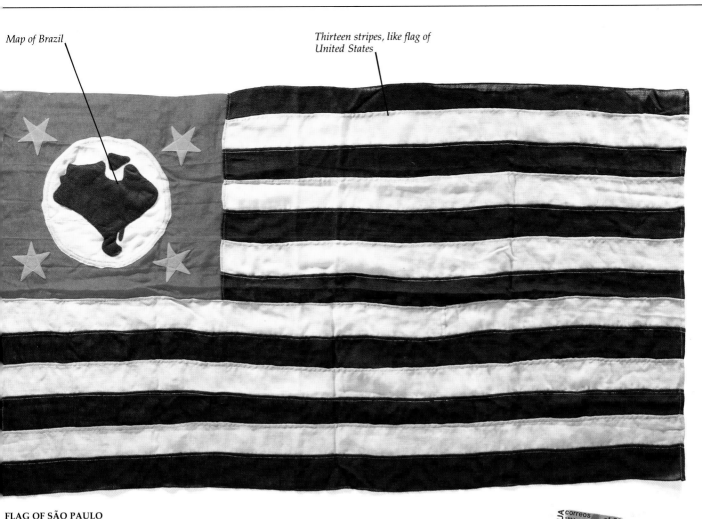

Map of Brazil

Thirteen stripes, like flag of United States

FLAG OF SÃO PAULO

[São] Paulo was one of the Brazilian [state]s which took a leading part in [the c]reation of the republic in 1888. [This fla]g, inspired in part by the [Stars] and Stripes, was one of several [prop]osed flags for the new republic - [with] the outline map of Brazil. It [was l]egally adopted as the state [flag i]n 1948. Many other new [desig]ns were proposed for Brazil, [but e]ventually the republic kept the [old fl]ag (p. 60).

Venezuela

Brazil

These pennants show the colors of Venezuela (the yellow, red, and blue of Miranda) and of Brazil (the green adopted on independence).

A BOLD STAND
The Brazilian flag in the Battle of Sam-Borja, 1865, during the war with Paraguay. The flag is green with the central arms in gold.

Stamp showing flag of Paraguay

WHICH FLAG?
This Nicaraguan stamp shows the flag of Puerto Rico.

CHARITABLE FLAG
Made by the women of the English colony at Rosario, Argentina, this flag bears the signatures of 750 subscribers to a fund to aid wounded soldiers of World War I.

Russia

MEETING OF ALLIES
This painting commem-
orating the alliance
between France and
Russia in 1893 shows
several pre-
revolutionary flags.

Bᴇғᴏʀᴇ ᴛʜᴇ ʀᴜssɪᴀɴ ʀᴇᴠᴏʟᴜᴛɪᴏɴ in 1917,
the person who had the greatest influence over the flags of Russia was the
emperor, Peter the Great. Among the
many things he did, Peter founded a navy
and endowed it with flags and ensigns.
These were based on Dutch models and
used the colors red, white, and blue.
These colors had been used on flags before
his reign, but he was the first to establish and
arrange a complete set of naval flags using these colors. Several other
Eastern European countries followed suit and adopted red, white and blue
flags. Many other flags were used in Russia before the revolution. During
World War I, for example, the civil flag had a yellow canton with the imperial
arms, but this was dropped in March
1917, before the revolution, when the
red flag of the communists took over.
During the revolution red flags with
inscriptions were widely used;
more traditional
ones were intro-
duced once the
new regime was
established.

P
THE G
This emperor re
from 1682 to 172
founded a nav
created the fl
Imperial R

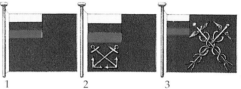

1 2 3

4 5 6 7

8 9 10 11

TO EACH HIS
Before and after the revolution R
had flags for every offic
department of govern
A selection is shown here. 1
Auxiliaries. 2 Finnish Customs
3 Customs Service. 4 Vice-Adr
5 Chief of Naval
6 Port Comma
7 Minister of
8 Hydrogr
Service. 9 I
Prin
. General-Adr
10 Czarev
General-Adr
11 General-Adr

OFF TO THE WAR
General Dragomiroff, who left Russia
for the war against Japan in 1904, kissed
the Russian flag as a sign of allegiance.
Pictures of soldiers kissing the flag were
popular patriotic images (p. 28).

RED ON SILVER
Diplomats often attach
flags to cars they use
abroad, for instant
recognition. Here, the
red flag of the former
Soviet Union flies from
the "Silver Lady" of an
English Rolls Royce.

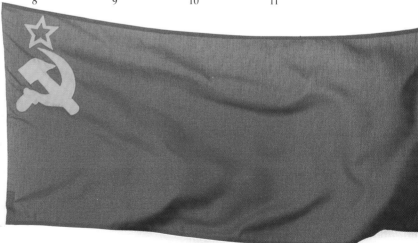

THE HAMMER AND SICKLE
Following the Russian Revolution, the Union of Soviet Socialist
Republics (USSR) was formed and remained in existence from 1922
until the Union break-up of 1991. The 15 republics in the Union
all used red flags based on the national flag, introduced in 1923.
The hammer and sickle represented the workers in industry and
agriculture, and the red star the guiding light of the Communist Party.

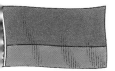

Byelorussia

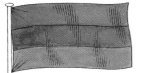

Armenia

Azerbaijan

Georgia

Ukraine

Moldova

PRE-SOVIET STATES
Before the formation of the Soviet Union, many separate states had been set up in the former Russian Empire. Their flags re-emerged as they regained independence after the August *coup* of 1991.

REGAINING A NAME
As the Communist structure crumbled, the people of Leningrad in the Russian republic decided once more to call their city St. Petersburg. This name was given to it by Peter the Great, but in 1924 the city had been re-named after V I Lenin, founder of the Communist party.

Tajikistan

Uzbekistan

Kyrgyzstan

Symbol of the sun and the felt tents of ancient nomads

CENTRAL ASIAN RENAISSANCE
The five states of central Asia are Moslem, but did not exist in their present boundaries until they became part of the Russian empire. Now they are fully independent, all their emblems are new.

RETURN OF THE TRICOLOUR
Following the *coup* and the disintegration of the USSR into independent states, the white, blue and red tricolor was re-adopted by Russia.

Turkmenistan

Kazakhstan

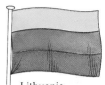

Latvia

Estonia

Lithuania

BALTIC STATES
The independence of the three Baltic states was recognised immediately after the *coup*. The flags which they had used before being forced into the Soviet Union were displayed once more.

China

IN CHINESE THOUGHT the world is divided into five parts: the center (colored yellow), the south (red), the the north (black), the west (white), and the east (blue). Each part has its own symbol - the dragon, for example, represents the east. So when in 1872 the Chinese at last adopted a national flag, it was natural that it should be yellow, for the "Middle Kingdom," and bear the Blue Dragon of the East. Yellow was also the color of the Manchu dynasty. In 1911, when revolutionaries within the army took over, the main flag took the form of five simple stripes in the traditional colors. This remained in use until 1928 when the flag of the Kuomintang party was adopted; it represented a white sun in blue sky over red land. This flag is still in use in Taiwan (p. 63), but was replaced on the mainland in 1949 by the red flag of the People's Republic.

EARLY ADVERTISEMENTS
Chinese traders' banners have carried inscriptions for centuries, as these examples show.

ALL ABOARD
This Chinese man carries the flag of the main Chinese shipping line. It was probably the Chinese flag most often seen by foreigners before 1911.

Cream silk

Painted figures

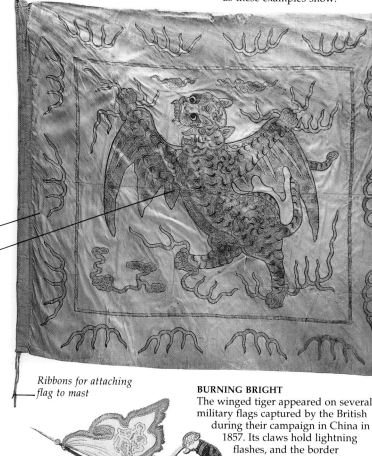

DRAGON OF THE EAST
This beautifully embroidered flag was the first form of the Chinese national flag, used from 1872 to 1890. The device of the blue dragon snapping at the sun was later used on a rectangular flag. The size of the flag varied with the size of the vessel, and could be up to 10 ft (3 m) long at the base.

Hand-embroidered silk

Ribbons for attaching flag to mast

The second form of the Chinese flag is shown in this image dating from 1894.

BURNING BRIGHT
The winged tiger appeared on several military flags captured by the British during their campaign in China in 1857. Its claws hold lightning flashes, and the border represents tongues of flame. The divisions of the Chinese army were known as banners.

Large star stands
for communism

Small star for one of
the four classes of society

The flag is 2:3 in proportion, and the
exact layout of the stars has been
specified. The large star is three
times the size of the small ones, and
one point of each of these is aimed
at the center of the large one.

Red field for
revolution

THE FLAG OF REVOLUTION
The red of the flag adopted in 1949
represents revolution, but also recalls the
color of the Han dynasty (206 B.C. - A.D. 220).
The large star represents com-
munism, and the four small ones
stand for the workers, peasants,
middle class, and "patriotic
capitalists."

JUNK FLAG
This early version
of the dragon flag
was taken from a
Chinese junk (sail-
boat) during the
Opium Wars
in the 19th
century.

Linen
hoist
with
tie
ribbons

FORCES FOR CHANGE *above*
This postage stamp shows
the flag of the Chinese
Liberation Army. The
characters on the flag stand
for 8-1, representing August 1,
1928, the date of the
army's formation.

ON THE MARCH
Sailors march through Beijing
carrying large, plain red flags.

Indented edge
typical of Chinese flags

Flags of all nations

TODAY'S NATIONAL FLAGS have a great variety of designs. On the following pages, 160 of the most interesting are shown, arranged by continent. There are many similarities between the different flags. A number of African countries use the colors red, yellow, green, and black, often known as "Pan-African colors." Arab countries often use red, white, black, and green. There are also flags derived from the French *Tricolore*, from the Stars and Stripes, and from the Crescent and Star flag of Turkey. National flags vary in shape, from the square Swiss flag to the long, thin flag of Qatar.

FLAGS OF THE WORLD
This illustration shows the variety of flags in use in the 19th century.

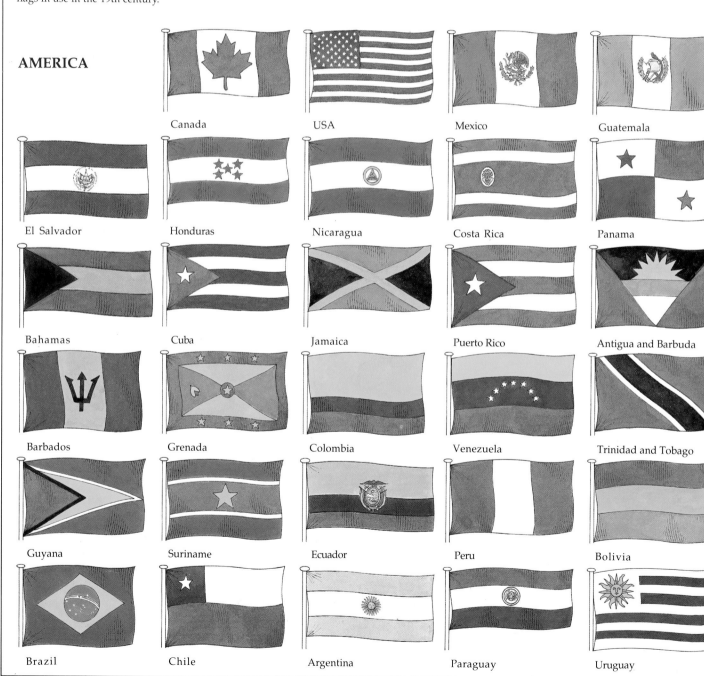

AMERICA

Canada

USA

Mexico

Guatemala

El Salvador

Honduras

Nicaragua

Costa Rica

Panama

Bahamas

Cuba

Jamaica

Puerto Rico

Antigua and Barbuda

Barbados

Grenada

Colombia

Venezuela

Trinidad and Tobago

Guyana

Suriname

Ecuador

Peru

Bolivia

Brazil

Chile

Argentina

Paraguay

Uruguay

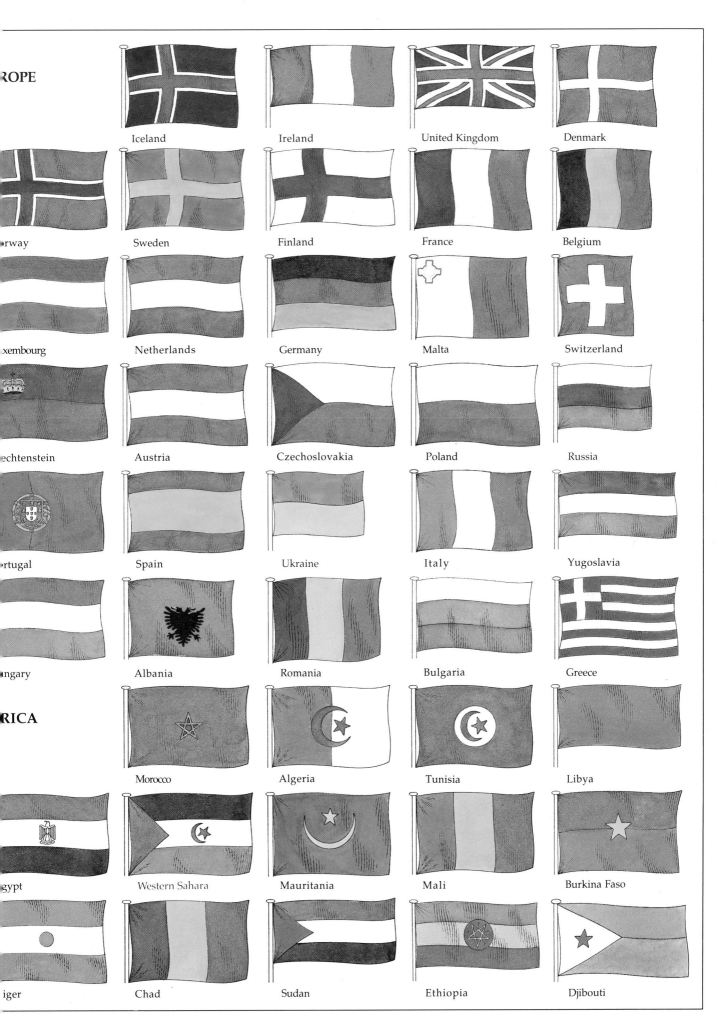

EUROPE

| Iceland | Ireland | United Kingdom | Denmark |

Norway | Sweden | Finland | France | Belgium

Luxembourg | Netherlands | Germany | Malta | Switzerland

Liechtenstein | Austria | Czechoslovakia | Poland | Russia

Portugal | Spain | Ukraine | Italy | Yugoslavia

Hungary | Albania | Romania | Bulgaria | Greece

AFRICA

Morocco | Algeria | Tunisia | Libya

Egypt | Western Sahara | Mauritania | Mali | Burkina Faso

Niger | Chad | Sudan | Ethiopia | Djibouti

Somalia

Senegal

Gambia

Guinea-Bissau

Guinea

Sierra Leone

Liberia

Côte d'Ivoire

Ghana

Togo

Benin

Nigeria

Cameroon

Central African Rep.

Equatorial Guinea

Gabon

Congo

Democratic Rep.
of Congo (Zaire)

Uganda

Kenya

Namibia

Burundi

Tanzania

Angola

Zambia

Malawi

Mozambique

Comoros

Botswana

Zimbabwe

South Africa

Lesotho

Swaziland

Madagascar

Mauritius

ASIA

Turkey

Israel

Lebanon

Syria

Jordan

Iraq

Saudi Arabia

Kuwait

Bahrain

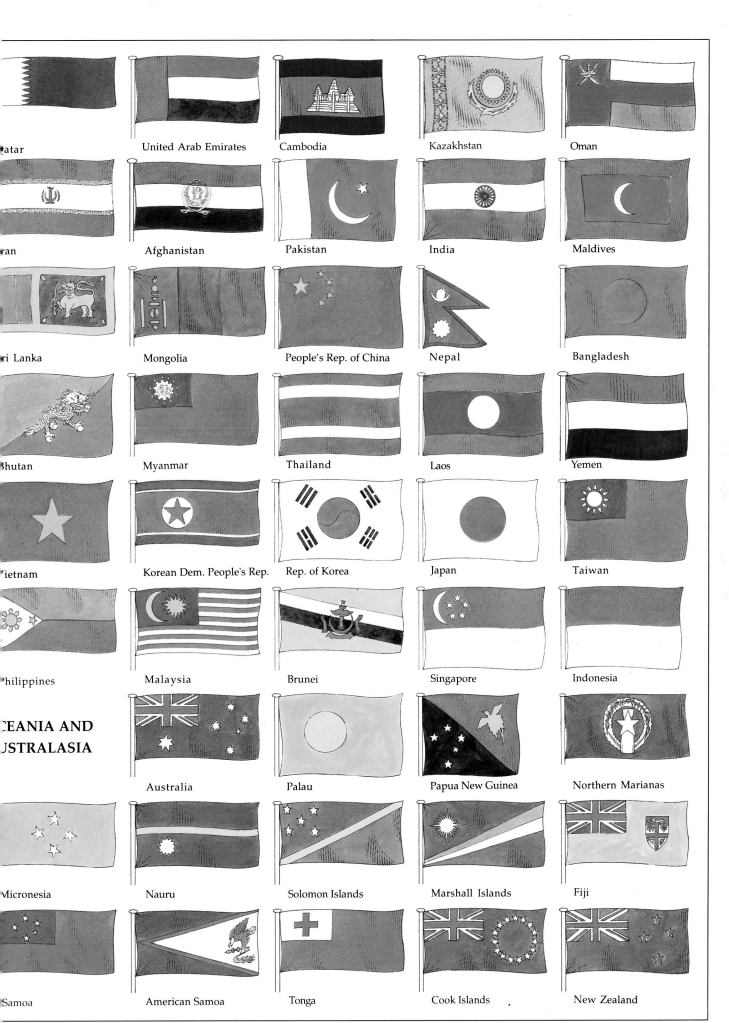

Qatar | United Arab Emirates | Cambodia | Kazakhstan | Oman

Iran | Afghanistan | Pakistan | India | Maldives

Sri Lanka | Mongolia | People's Rep. of China | Nepal | Bangladesh

Bhutan | Myanmar | Thailand | Laos | Yemen

Vietnam | Korean Dem. People's Rep. | Rep. of Korea | Japan | Taiwan

Philippines | Malaysia | Brunei | Singapore | Indonesia

OCEANIA AND AUSTRALASIA

Australia | Palau | Papua New Guinea | Northern Marianas

Micronesia | Nauru | Solomon Islands | Marshall Islands | Fiji

Samoa | American Samoa | Tonga | Cook Islands | New Zealand

Index

Acknowledgments

Dorling Kindersley would like to thank:
For providing flags and other artifacts for photography: Barbara Tomlinson, David Spence, Jim Stephenson, and the staff of the National Maritime Museum; Sylvia Hopkins and the staff of the National Army Museum; Sybil Burnaby and the staff of the Heralds' Museum; the College of Arms; the Royal Hospital of Saint Bartholomew; River Mill Flags; Turtle and Pearce Ltd; Black and Edgington Flags; Newitt and Co; John Eagle; the Flag Institute. J. P. Brooke-Little and R. C.

Yorke for information on heraldry. Ray Allen of the Imperial War Museum for information and photographs. Vicky Davenport for advice on the planning of the book. Miranda Kennedy and Richard Czapnik for design assistance. Meryl Silbert. Fred Ford of Radius Graphics for paste-up

Photographers Karl Shone, Martin Plomer
Illustrators John Woodcock, Will Giles
Picture research Stasz Gnych, Angela Murphy

Picture credits
t=top b=bottom m=middle l=left r=right

Bibliothèque Nationale, Paris: 10 br
Bridgeman Art Library: 16tl, 17mr, 18m, 19bl, 26t, 26ml, 26br, 36ml, 46tr, 46mr, 49bl, 52tr, 54tr
British Museum: 8tl, 12cl, 36tr
Camera Press: 18br, 21m, 21br, 25bl, 28tl, 32mr, 32bm, 32br, 33bl, 38m, 38bl
College of Arms: 10mr, 11tl, 18tl
Colorsport: 20tl, 20tr, 20br, 54b
Mary Evans Picture Library: 7tl, 7tr, 9tl, 13c, 14m, 22tl, 22mr, 24tl, 30ml, 30mr, 32bl, 36bl, 36br, 39bl, 44ml, 46bl, 47bl, 50tl, 56tl, 56ml, 54m, 55bl, 58bl
GAMMA: 37br
Susan Griggs Agency: 34br, 35mr
Michael Holford: 8bl, 12tl

Robert Hunt: 13mr, 13tl, 17bl, 19m, 23tr, 24tr, 24m, 28br, 29bl, 34ml, 46mr, 52br, 57mr, 57bl
Imperial War Museum: 13br, 24mr, 28bl, 29br, 30tl, 47br, 55br
Popperfoto: 6tr, 42bl
Rex Features/SIPA Press: 19tl, 41bm, 44br, 47ml, 51bl, 53br, 57ml, 59br
Science Photo Library/NASA: 25br
Frank Spooner Pictures: 18ml, 24br, 30bl, 31b, 50br
TRH/Tass: 23m
US National Archives: 25m

DORLING KINDERSLEY EYEWITNESS BOOKS

1. BIRD
2. ROCKS & MINERALS
3. SKELETON
4. ARMS & ARMOR
5. TREE
6. POND & RIVER
7. BUTTERFLY & MOTH
8. SPORTS
9. SHELL
10. EARLY HUMANS
11. MAMMAL
12. MUSIC
13. DINOSAUR
14. PLANT
15. SEASHORE
16. FLAG
17. INSECT
18. MONEY
19. FOSSIL
20. FISH
21. CAR
22. FLYING MACHINE
23. ANCIENT EGYPT
24. ANCIENT ROME
25. CRYSTAL & GEM
26. REPTILE
27. INVENTION
28. WEATHER
29. CAT
30. BIBLE LANDS
31. EXPLORER
32. DOG
33. HORSE
34. FILM
35. COSTUME
36. BOAT
37. ANCIENT GREECE
38. VOLCANO & EARTHQUAKE
39. TRAIN
40. SHARK
41. AMPHIBIAN
42. ELEPHANT
43. KNIGHT
44. MUMMY
45. COWBOY
46. WHALE
47. AZTEC, INCA & MAYA
48. BOOK
49. CASTLE
50. VIKING
51. DESERT
52. PREHISTORIC LIFE
53. PYRAMID
54. JUNGLE
55. ANCIENT CHINA